Part I: The End of the Ice Age and the Younger Dryas

Chapter 1: Introduction: The Ice Age and Its End

Overview of the Ice Age

The Ice Age, or more accurately the **Pleistocene Epoch**, refers to a period in Earth's history that spanned from about 2.6 million years ago to approximately 11,700 years ago. During this time, large portions of the Earth's surface were covered by massive ice sheets and glaciers. This epoch was marked by repeated glacial cycles, where ice sheets advanced and retreated, significantly influencing the Earth's climate, ecosystems, and sea levels. These cycles of glaciation are often referred to as **"ice ages"**, and there have been multiple ice ages throughout Earth's history, but the Pleistocene is the most recent and the one that directly precedes the Holocene, the current interglacial period.

The Pleistocene Glaciations

The Ice Age was characterized by a series of glaciations, during which temperatures dropped dramatically, and glaciers expanded from the poles toward lower latitudes. The most significant glaciations during the Pleistocene include:

1. **The Early Glaciations** (around 2.6 million to 800,000 years ago): These were some of the first large-scale glaciations, which set the stage for the alternating warm and cold periods that would follow.

2. **The Last Glacial Maximum (LGM)** (approximately 20,000 years ago): This represents the peak of the most recent ice age. During the LGM, ice sheets covered vast portions of North America, Europe, and Asia, with sea levels around 120 meters lower than present. Temperatures were much colder than today, and many species of megafauna, such as mammoths and saber-toothed cats, flourished in the frigid environment.

The glaciers during the Ice Age acted as massive forces, reshaping the landscape, carving out valleys, fjords, and mountain ranges, and influencing the flow of rivers and ocean currents. These glaciers also contributed to significant climatic shifts, often creating colder, drier conditions in some regions while promoting more humid environments in others.

The Transition to the Holocene

The transition from the Pleistocene to the **Holocene** (the current geological epoch) around 11,700 years ago marks the end of the last Ice Age. This transition was not an instantaneous event but a gradual shift in global climate, where Earth's temperature began to rise, and the ice sheets began to recede. The warming of the Earth was driven by a complex set of factors, including:

- **Changes in Earth's orbit and axial tilt** (Milankovitch cycles), which altered the distribution of solar energy across the planet.
- **Increased greenhouse gas concentrations**, particularly carbon dioxide (CO_2) and methane (CH_4), which enhanced the greenhouse effect and led to global warming.
- **The deglaciation process**, where the massive ice sheets began melting, contributing to rising sea levels and changing ecosystems.

The end of the Ice Age brought significant changes in global ecosystems. Temperate forests expanded in many regions, while tundra and ice-covered landscapes retreated. The megafauna that had once roamed the Earth began to die off, likely due to a combination of climate change, habitat loss, and human hunting pressures.

The Younger Dryas Period: A Cold Reversal

Although the planet was generally warming at the end of the Pleistocene, **the Younger Dryas** period, occurring roughly between 12,800 and 11,700 years ago, represents an abrupt climatic reversal. It is characterized by a sudden return to near-glacial conditions, even as the Earth had been warming and transitioning toward the Holocene.

The Younger Dryas is often referred to as a **"century-scale cold snap"**, where temperatures in the Northern Hemisphere dropped dramatically, and the climate became much colder and drier. In some areas, such as the North Atlantic, temperatures may have plummeted by as much as 15°C (27°F) within a short period. This sharp cooling is believed to have been caused by disruptions to the global ocean circulation, particularly the **Atlantic Meridional Overturning Circulation (AMOC)**, which is a crucial component of the Earth's climate system.

The cause of the Younger Dryas cooling event is still a topic of debate, with the leading hypothesis being that a **comet or asteroid impact** triggered this abrupt change. This theory suggests that the impact, or series of impacts, released vast amounts of debris into the atmosphere, blocking sunlight and cooling the planet. Other theories include the disruption of ocean currents due to the massive influx of freshwater from the melting Laurentide Ice Sheet, or significant volcanic activity.

The Younger Dryas and Global Impact

The Younger Dryas had significant consequences for both the climate and the ecosystems of the Earth. In North America, for example, the cooling event coincided with the **extinction of many megafauna species**, such as mammoths, mastodons, and saber-toothed cats. Many of these species had been thriving during the warmer Pleistocene, but the sudden onset of cold conditions and the disruption of their ecosystems may have led to their rapid extinction.

In Europe, the climate reversal would have had similar effects on human populations and animal species. Archaeological evidence suggests that prehistoric human cultures were forced to adapt to the changing conditions, with some groups migrating to more favorable environments, while others faced famine and collapse.

The transition out of the Younger Dryas and into the Holocene was equally dramatic. Once the cooling event ended around 11,700 years ago, the Earth began to warm rapidly again, leading to the stabilizing of modern climatic conditions. This shift allowed for the development of human civilizations and the rise of agriculture, which marks the dawn of the **Neolithic Revolution**.

The end of the Ice Age was a pivotal moment in Earth's history, marking the transition from a frozen, glacial world to a warmer, more temperate climate. This shift, which included the abrupt cooling of the Younger Dryas period, set the stage for the rise of human civilizations and the development of agriculture. The echoes of this cataclysmic event are still present in the collective memories of ancient cultures, which may have passed down stories of great floods and disasters that reflected the upheavals of their time.

Understanding the Ice Age's end, the Younger Dryas, and their associated catastrophes provides important context for exploring the connections between ancient mythologies and real-world events. In the next chapters, we will explore how the catastrophic events of this time, including potential impacts and the subsequent environmental upheaval, may have been recorded and passed down as global flood myths.

Chapter 2: The Younger Dryas Impact Hypothesis

Introduction to the Younger Dryas Impact Hypothesis

The **Younger Dryas Impact Hypothesis** proposes that a cosmic event—specifically, the impact of a comet or asteroid—triggered the abrupt and extreme climate reversal that occurred around 12,800 years ago, marking the beginning of the **Younger Dryas** period. This theory suggests that the impact (or multiple impacts) released massive amounts of debris and particulate matter into the Earth's atmosphere, which led to a dramatic cooling event that reversed the warming trend at the end of the last Ice Age. This hypothesis is supported by a combination of **geological evidence**, **climate data**, and **archaeological findings** that suggest a global cataclysm, including the extinction of megafauna, the decline of early human cultures, and the disruption of ecosystems.

The Younger Dryas is one of the most mysterious and significant climatic events in Earth's history, and understanding its causes is crucial for uncovering how rapid climate change has affected life on Earth. The theory of a cosmic impact provides a compelling explanation for the sudden onset of the Younger Dryas cold snap, which coincided with mass extinctions and upheaval in both natural environments and human societies.

Background: The Younger Dryas Period

The Younger Dryas refers to an abrupt return to near-glacial conditions in the Northern Hemisphere, following the general warming at the end of the Ice Age. Before the Younger Dryas, Earth was transitioning from the Pleistocene Epoch into the Holocene (the current interglacial period). The warming of the Earth began approximately 14,000 years ago, but around 12,800 years ago, temperatures suddenly dropped, leading to a cold snap that lasted for about 1,200 years, until around 11,700 years ago.

The event was particularly pronounced in the North Atlantic region but had significant global consequences. It has been suggested that the rapid cooling was triggered by the disruption of ocean currents, particularly the **Atlantic Meridional Overturning Circulation (AMOC)**, which plays a key role in regulating global climate. The hypothesis proposes that this disruption was caused by an influx of freshwater into the North Atlantic, potentially from the sudden melting of ice sheets. However, an alternative and increasingly accepted theory is that the Younger Dryas was caused by a cosmic impact, which would have added another layer of complexity to the environmental changes already underway.

The Cosmic Impact Hypothesis

The core idea of the Younger Dryas Impact Hypothesis is that a **comet or asteroid** struck Earth around 12,800 years ago, causing a **global catastrophe** that triggered the abrupt cooling of the Younger Dryas period. This theory posits that the impact, or impacts, released an enormous amount of energy, which resulted in several dramatic environmental changes:

1. **The Release of Dust and Soot into the Atmosphere**: The impact(s) would have caused large-scale fires, igniting forests and grasslands. The resulting soot and ash would have been ejected into the atmosphere, blocking sunlight and leading to a **global cooling** effect. This "nuclear winter"-like scenario could have caused temperatures to drop rapidly, particularly in the Northern Hemisphere, contributing to the abrupt onset of the Younger Dryas.

2. **Massive Disruption of Ocean Circulation**: The impact would have melted large portions of the ice sheets, releasing **freshwater** into the North Atlantic. This sudden influx of freshwater would have disrupted the delicate balance of the **Atlantic Meridional Overturning Circulation (AMOC)**, a key component of the global ocean conveyor belt. The AMOC is responsible for transporting warm water from the equator toward the North Atlantic, and any disruption would have led to a cooling of the Northern Hemisphere.

3. **Impact Debris and Firestorms**: The cosmic object itself, whether a comet or asteroid, would have exploded in the atmosphere or struck the Earth's surface, creating firestorms and further adding to the

atmospheric debris. This debris would have created a prolonged period of reduced sunlight, lowering temperatures and destabilizing ecosystems.

4. **A Chain Reaction of Environmental Catastrophes**: The combination of cooling temperatures, atmospheric disruption, and fires would have had cascading effects on ecosystems and climates worldwide. In addition to temperature drops, there would have been a sharp decline in vegetation, disruption of the food chain, and significant changes in precipitation patterns. These changes would have caused **mass extinctions** of megafauna, such as mammoths, mastodons, and saber-toothed cats, and the collapse of early human cultures that depended on these species for food and resources.

Evidence Supporting the Impact Hypothesis

The Younger Dryas Impact Hypothesis is supported by several lines of evidence, although it remains controversial. The key pieces of evidence that suggest a cosmic event played a role in the onset of the Younger Dryas include:

1. **Iridium and Nanodiamonds**: One of the primary pieces of evidence comes from the discovery of **iridium**, a rare metal typically associated with extraterrestrial objects, and **nanodiamonds**, which are often formed under high-pressure conditions such as those found during an impact. Both of these have been found in sediment layers dated to the time of the Younger Dryas, specifically in locations across North America and Europe. The presence of these materials suggests that an impact or series of impacts occurred around 12,800 years ago.

2. **Carbon Soot and Charcoal**: Sediment cores from various sites, particularly in North America, contain significant quantities of **charcoal and carbon soot**, which suggest widespread fires at the time of the Younger Dryas. These fires would have been ignited by the heat and energy released by the impact(s), supporting the hypothesis that a cosmic event caused massive environmental disruptions.

3. **Climatic and Ecological Disruptions**: The Younger Dryas cooling event itself is one of the strongest pieces of evidence for an external cause, as the rapid temperature drop does not appear to have been

caused by typical Earthly mechanisms such as volcanic eruptions or gradual shifts in Earth's orbit. The cooling, which occurred within a matter of decades, is far more abrupt than the typical fluctuations in Earth's climate.

4. **Mass Extinctions of Megafauna**: The timing of the megafaunal extinctions in North America and other regions coincides with the onset of the Younger Dryas. The large, slow-moving megafauna that had thrived during the Ice Age were decimated, possibly due to the sudden cold snap, loss of habitat, and disruption of food sources. This aligns with the idea that a sudden, catastrophic event would have been devastating to these species.

5. **Geological Evidence of Impact Sites**: Researchers have identified potential impact sites, such as **the Hiawatha Crater** in Greenland, that could be related to the Younger Dryas. These impact sites may have been responsible for the significant environmental changes observed at the time. However, the identification of a specific, definitive impact site remains a subject of ongoing research.

Challenges and Criticisms of the Hypothesis

Despite the growing body of supporting evidence, the Younger Dryas Impact Hypothesis has faced significant criticism and skepticism from some in the scientific community. Some of the key criticisms include:

1. **Lack of Clear Impact Evidence**: While there is evidence of extraterrestrial materials like iridium and nanodiamonds, there is no clear evidence of a large impact crater directly linked to the Younger Dryas. Some researchers argue that the evidence may be circumstantial and that alternative explanations, such as volcanic eruptions or natural environmental fluctuations, might account for the observed changes.

2. **Competing Theories**: Other scientists argue that the Younger Dryas cooling was caused by the release of freshwater from the melting ice sheets, which disrupted the global ocean circulation. This hypothesis suggests that the North Atlantic cooling occurred due to changes in the salinity and density of ocean water, rather than a cosmic impact.

3. **Global Firestorms**: Some critics question the idea that firestorms of the scale proposed by the impact hypothesis would have occurred, as the necessary conditions for such widespread fires are still debated. Additionally, some studies suggest that the charcoal evidence may be linked to more mundane natural causes, such as wildfires that were not directly related to an extraterrestrial impact.

The **Younger Dryas Impact Hypothesis** remains one of the most intriguing explanations for one of the most abrupt climate changes in Earth's history. While it is not universally accepted, the evidence supporting the idea of a cosmic impact causing the Younger Dryas provides a compelling narrative for the global catastrophe that affected Earth's ecosystems and human populations. As research continues, the Younger Dryas Impact Hypothesis could offer new insights into the role of cosmic events in shaping the planet's history and the evolution of life. The connection between this event and ancient flood myths may offer even further clues into how humanity has remembered this cataclysmic event across cultures.

Chapter 3: Evidence of the Cataclysm

The **Younger Dryas Impact Hypothesis** posits that a cosmic event, likely a comet or asteroid impact, triggered a cataclysmic climate shift around 12,800 years ago, plunging Earth into the cold conditions of the Younger Dryas. In order to support this hypothesis, a variety of **geological** and **archaeological** evidence has been uncovered, which strongly suggests that a significant and sudden event—likely involving an impact—took place, reshaping Earth's ecosystems, climate, and the course of human history. This chapter will delve into the specific lines of evidence that provide support for the hypothesis, including the discovery of **nanodiamonds**, **meltwater pulses**, and other geological anomalies that hint at an extraterrestrial cause for the Younger Dryas cooling.

1. Nanodiamonds: Traces of Cosmic Impacts

One of the most compelling pieces of evidence for the Younger Dryas Impact Hypothesis is the discovery of **nanodiamonds** in sedimentary layers dating to around 12,800 years ago. These diamonds are microscopic in size, often measured in nanometers (billionths of a meter), and are typically formed under the intense pressure and heat associated with cosmic impacts or explosions.

Where and How Nanodiamonds Were Found:
Nanodiamonds have been discovered in **sediment cores** from several sites around the world, including locations in **North America, Europe**, and **Greenland**. These samples were taken from layers of sediment that were deposited at the time of the Younger Dryas, specifically at the boundary between the **Pleistocene** and **Holocene** epochs. Researchers studying these layers have found an **unusual concentration of nanodiamonds** and other **exotic materials**, such as **fullerenes** (molecules composed of carbon atoms arranged in a structure similar to a soccer ball) and **graphitic carbon**, which also point to a high-energy cosmic event.

The **formation of nanodiamonds** requires extremely high pressures, such as those generated during an impact event. Natural processes like volcanic eruptions or lightning strikes do not typically produce such diamonds, making their presence in these layers difficult to explain without the occurrence of a comet or asteroid strike. The discovery of nanodiamonds is significant because they provide a **signature of extraterrestrial material** that aligns with the hypothesis of a cosmic event causing the Younger Dryas.

Implications for the Impact Hypothesis:
The presence of nanodiamonds in the Younger Dryas boundary layers suggests that a **cosmic object**, such as a **comet** or **asteroid**, either exploded in the atmosphere or impacted the Earth's surface, releasing enough energy to create these diamonds. These particles would have been widely dispersed across the globe, contributing to the catastrophic events that followed, such as global fires, cooling, and massive disruptions to ecosystems.

2. Iridium: Evidence of Extraterrestrial Material

Another key line of evidence supporting the impact hypothesis is the discovery of **iridium** in sediment layers dating to the Younger Dryas. Iridium is a rare metal that is more commonly found in **meteorites** and **comets** than in the Earth's crust. Its presence in **large quantities** in the sedimentary layers at the Younger Dryas boundary strongly suggests that an **extraterrestrial object**—likely a comet or asteroid—collided with Earth or exploded in the atmosphere around 12,800 years ago.

Where Iridium Has Been Found:
Iridium has been identified in sediment cores taken from multiple regions, including **North America, Europe**, and **Greenland**, which aligns with the idea of a **global event**. This distribution of iridium points to the possibility of a large, significant impact or a series of impacts that would have scattered this material over vast distances.

Iridium and Nanodiamonds:
The presence of both **iridium** and **nanodiamonds** in the same sediment layers is particularly compelling because they are both associated with high-energy cosmic events. While iridium suggests an extraterrestrial source, nanodiamonds support the idea of an intense impact event that would have generated the extreme pressures necessary for their formation. These findings strengthen the connection between the Younger Dryas cooling and a cosmic impact.

3. Meltwater Pulses and Disrupted Ocean Currents

In addition to the evidence of extraterrestrial material, the Younger Dryas Impact Hypothesis is also supported by the geological phenomenon known as **meltwater pulses**. These pulses refer to the rapid release of large quantities of freshwater into the ocean, which would have disrupted ocean currents and significantly altered Earth's climate. It is widely believed that the influx of meltwater during the late Pleistocene contributed to the abrupt cooling of the Younger Dryas.

The Role of Ice Sheets:
At the time of the Younger Dryas, **massive ice sheets** covered much of North America, Europe, and Asia. The **Laurentide Ice Sheet** in North America and the **Fennoscandian Ice Sheet** in Europe were melting due to warming temperatures at the end of the Ice Age. As these ice sheets began to melt more rapidly, vast amounts of **freshwater** were released into the **Atlantic Ocean**, particularly into the **North Atlantic**.

The sudden influx of freshwater from melting glaciers could have interfered with the **Atlantic Meridional Overturning Circulation (AMOC)**, a vital oceanic current system that helps regulate global temperatures by transporting warm water from the equator toward the North Pole. The disruption of the AMOC likely caused a dramatic cooling in the Northern Hemisphere, leading to the onset of the Younger Dryas.

Possible Connection to the Impact:
One theory suggests that the impact of a comet or asteroid could have **accelerated the melting of ice sheets** by producing enough heat to trigger the rapid disintegration of ice, releasing freshwater into the oceans. The **disruption of the AMOC** would have led to the cooling of the Northern Hemisphere, a process that aligns with the abrupt temperature drop characteristic of the Younger Dryas.

4. Evidence of Global Wildfires

Another key piece of evidence that supports the Younger Dryas Impact Hypothesis is the discovery of **charcoal** and **soot** in the Younger Dryas boundary layers. These materials indicate that **wildfires** occurred at a **global scale** around the time of the impact, which would have been ignited by the heat and shockwaves produced by the cosmic event.

Where Wildfire Evidence Has Been Found:
Charcoal and soot have been found in sediment layers in **North America**, **Europe**, and **Asia**, which suggests that wildfires affected large regions across the Northern Hemisphere. These fires likely occurred in **grasslands, forests**, and other ecosystems that were struck by the heat and debris from the cosmic event. The widespread nature of these fires suggests that they were the result of a **single catastrophic event**, rather than a series of smaller, localized fires.

Link to Impact Hypothesis:
The heat produced by the explosion of a comet or asteroid, or the subsequent firestorms, would have ignited extensive wildfires, contributing to the release of soot and charcoal into the atmosphere. The smoke and particulate matter would have further reduced the amount of sunlight reaching the Earth's surface, intensifying the cooling effect and contributing to the global climate disruption associated with the Younger Dryas.

5. Megafaunal Extinctions and Human Displacement

The climatic shifts and environmental disruptions caused by the Younger Dryas would have had catastrophic effects on both ecosystems and human populations. During this time, many **megafauna species**, including mammoths, mastodons, and saber-toothed cats, went extinct. The abrupt cooling, habitat loss, and disruption of food chains are believed to have contributed to these extinctions. Additionally, the impact event may have altered human migration patterns and forced early human populations to adapt to rapidly changing conditions.

Link to Impact Hypothesis:
The timing of the **megafaunal extinctions** and the **decline of early human cultures** aligns with the abrupt climatic changes caused by the Younger Dryas. The environmental cataclysm associated with the impact would have been a key factor in the disappearance of these species and the alteration of human societies.

The evidence supporting the Younger Dryas Impact Hypothesis comes from multiple, independent lines of inquiry, including the discovery of **nanodiamonds, iridium, meltwater pulses, global wildfires**, and the **extinction of megafauna**. These pieces of evidence suggest that a **cosmic impact**—or a series of impacts—triggered the dramatic cooling of the Younger Dryas and had profound consequences for the Earth's climate, ecosystems, and early human societies. As research continues, it is likely that additional evidence will emerge to further confirm or refine this hypothesis, shedding light on one of the most significant and mysterious events in Earth's history.

Chapter 4: The Worldwide Climate Crisis

The **Younger Dryas** represents one of the most dramatic episodes of **climate change** in Earth's history, marked by an abrupt cooling event that had far-reaching consequences across the globe. This sudden climatic shift, which occurred around 12,800 years ago, is thought to have been triggered by a **cosmic impact**, causing widespread environmental disruption, mass extinctions, and the collapse of early human cultures. In this chapter, we will explore how the **global cooling** of the Younger Dryas period unfolded, the **mass extinctions** it precipitated, and the **cultural upheavals** that accompanied this environmental crisis.

1. The Abrupt Cooling Event

Before the onset of the Younger Dryas, the Earth was transitioning from the **Pleistocene** Ice Age into the warmer conditions of the **Holocene** epoch. This period, which began approximately 14,000 years ago, saw a gradual rise in temperatures as the last Ice Age glaciers began to retreat. However, around **12,800 years ago**, Earth's climate experienced an **abrupt and dramatic cooling** that brought a sharp reversal to this warming trend.

This sudden temperature drop, which is characteristic of the Younger Dryas, is one of the most extreme **climate fluctuations** in Earth's history. Within a matter of **decades** (or even years), temperatures in the Northern Hemisphere plummeted by as much as **10°C (18°F)**, with cold conditions persisting for over a thousand years. This cooling period lasted for approximately **1,200 years**, until around **11,700 years ago**, when the Earth finally entered the warmer Holocene epoch.

Global Climate Impact:
While the Younger Dryas cooling event was most pronounced in the **Northern Hemisphere**, it had significant global consequences. The disruption of ocean currents—especially the **Atlantic Meridional Overturning Circulation (AMOC)**, which helps regulate global temperatures—likely played a major role in amplifying the cooling. The cooling period disrupted **monsoon patterns**, leading to altered rainfall regimes in many parts of the world, including **Africa, Asia**, and the **Americas**. This caused widespread **droughts, desertification**, and a shift in the availability of natural resources that affected both ecosystems and human societies.

2. The Collapse of Ecosystems and Mass Extinctions

The abrupt cooling and environmental disruption caused by the Younger Dryas had a profound impact on Earth's **biota**—the vast array of plant and animal life that populated the planet. The cooling period is thought to have been a major factor in the **extinction of megafauna**—large animals that had flourished during the Ice Age but were poorly adapted to the rapidly changing climate.

Extinction of Megafauna:
Species such as **mammoths, mastodons, saber-toothed cats, giant ground sloths**, and **woolly rhinoceroses** were particularly vulnerable to

the sudden climatic shift. Many of these animals were already stressed by the **end of the Ice Age**, which brought significant changes to their habitats, as well as by hunting pressures from early human populations. The cold snap of the Younger Dryas exacerbated these stresses, leading to the extinction of numerous megafauna species.

1. **Climate-induced habitat loss**: As temperatures plummeted, vast areas of tundra and steppe—habitats crucial for these large animals—were replaced by **colder, less hospitable environments**, such as **forests** and **shrublands**, reducing food availability and disrupting migration patterns.

2. **Direct impact of the cold**: The extreme cold would have been lethal to many of these species, especially those that were adapted to more temperate or colder climates but could not survive the rapid, sustained cooling.

3. **Shifting ecosystems**: The sudden cooling would have disrupted the complex food chains in which the megafauna were at the top. Smaller herbivores and carnivores would have been equally affected, as they too depended on the ecosystems that were drastically altered by the temperature shifts.

The **extinctions** that occurred during this period were not confined to megafauna. Many smaller species, including birds, amphibians, and reptiles, were also affected by the shifting climates and habitats, leading to **local extinctions** and major shifts in biodiversity across continents.

A Global Event:
Evidence of these extinctions is not limited to any one region. Fossil records show that **North America**, **Europe**, and **Asia** all experienced similar declines in megafauna populations. In North America, the disappearance of **mammoths** and other large mammals is well-documented, while in Europe, **woolly rhinoceroses** and **giant deer** also vanished. In some cases, these extinctions were so sudden and severe that they have been interpreted as the result of a **catastrophic event**, such as an impact or series of impacts, rather than gradual climate change.

3. Cultural Upheavals and Human Responses

The abrupt climatic changes of the Younger Dryas also had far-reaching consequences for human societies, especially those that were already established at the time. The cooling period disrupted the **hunter-gatherer** societies that depended on megafauna for sustenance and survival. As the megafauna disappeared and environmental conditions deteriorated, these early human cultures were forced to adapt in drastic ways.

Human Displacement and Adaptation:

1. **Shift in Subsistence Strategies**: Many human groups that had relied on megafauna hunting had to shift their subsistence strategies. This might have led to increased reliance on **smaller game**, **plant foods**, and **fishing**. In regions affected by extreme cold, such as parts of **North America, Europe**, and **Asia**, this would have been a significant challenge, as food resources became scarcer and more unpredictable.

2. **Migration**: With their traditional hunting grounds becoming inhospitable, many human groups likely began migrating in search of more favorable conditions. Evidence suggests that humans may have moved toward more temperate climates or regions where they could find new resources. This migration could explain some of the patterns of human settlement that appear to have spread out from **Beringia** (the land bridge that connected Asia and North America) and other areas during the late Pleistocene and early Holocene.

3. **Cultural Disintegration**: For some societies, the Younger Dryas may have led to **cultural upheaval**. The collapse of early human cultures that were heavily reliant on megafauna and specific hunting practices could have resulted in the disintegration of established social structures. The disruption of the environment may also have led to **famine, conflict**, and **social unrest**, as human groups competed for dwindling resources.

Archaeological Evidence of Cultural Responses:

Archaeological evidence suggests that human societies during the Younger Dryas adapted in various ways to the changing conditions:

- **Technological Innovation**: Some human groups may have developed new tools and strategies to exploit the resources that were available to them, including the use of **microliths** (small, specialized stone tools) for hunting smaller game, or the development of **fishing techniques** to take advantage of aquatic resources.

- **Cave Art and Symbolism**: In some regions, the advent of the Younger Dryas corresponds with changes in **cave art** and symbolic expression. It is possible that the dramatic environmental changes inspired humans to express their **fears**, **myths**, and **spiritual beliefs** in ways that have been preserved in rock art.
- **Cultural Revival Post-Younger Dryas**: After the end of the Younger Dryas, human populations seemed to recover and adapt to the new environmental conditions. This period saw the development of early **agriculture**, particularly in the Near East, and the rise of settled societies, marking the transition from **hunter-gatherer** lifestyles to **agrarian** ones.

4. Global Effects on Ecosystems and Climate

The cooling period also had a significant impact on ecosystems across the globe:

1. **Disrupted Ecosystems**: The global cooling disrupted many ecosystems, pushing some species into **extinction**, while forcing others to adapt or migrate. Species that could not adjust to the cooler temperatures or the changes in vegetation and rainfall were more likely to disappear, leading to major shifts in biodiversity.

2. **Altered Vegetation Zones**: As temperatures dropped, vegetation zones also shifted. **Forest ecosystems** expanded into areas that had previously been dominated by **grasslands** and **tundra**, displacing species that were adapted to those environments. Similarly, **desertification** occurred in regions where rainfall patterns were altered, exacerbating the harsh living conditions for both animals and humans.

3. **Oceanic Changes**: The cooling event likely led to changes in **marine ecosystems**, with the disruption of **ocean currents** and temperature shifts affecting marine life. **Cold-water species** would have flourished, while warmer water species may have experienced declines.

The abrupt cooling of the Younger Dryas period caused by the **climate crisis** had widespread and long-lasting effects on Earth's ecosystems, species, and human cultures. The **mass extinctions** that followed reshaped the planet's biodiversity, and the **cultural upheavals** forced early human societies to adapt and evolve new ways of living. The legacy of the Younger Dryas is a reminder of how rapidly and dramatically **climate events** can disrupt the course of history. Understanding the impact of this crisis provides valuable insights into how future **climate change** could affect both the natural world and human societies.

Chapter 5: The Impact on North America: The Clovis Culture and Megafauna Extinction

The Younger Dryas, an abrupt climatic cooling event that occurred around 12,800 years ago, had profound effects on the environment of **North America**. Among the most significant consequences were the **extinction of megafauna**, such as **mammoths**, **mastodons**, and **giant ground sloths**, and the dramatic cultural shifts experienced by the **Clovis people**, the earliest known inhabitants of North America. In this chapter, we will explore how the **Clovis culture**—recognized for its distinct stone tools and hunting practices—was impacted by the Younger Dryas, and how the extinction of megafauna intersected with these cultural and ecological changes.

1. The Clovis Culture: A Snapshot

The **Clovis people** are often considered to be among the first humans to settle in North America, arriving around **13,000 years ago** or earlier, at the tail end of the **Pleistocene Epoch**. The Clovis culture is primarily defined by the distinctive **Clovis point**, a finely crafted stone spearpoint, which was used for hunting large game, particularly **megafauna**. The Clovis people were skilled **hunters-gatherers**, living in small, mobile bands, and they relied heavily on large animals like **mammoths**, **mastodons**, and **bison** for food, tools, and materials.

Clovis Toolkits:
The **Clovis toolkit** was versatile, consisting of various tools such as scrapers, knives, and projectile points, all made from **flint** or other stone materials. The **Clovis points**—large, **leaf-shaped**, and **fluted**

spearheads—were designed to be attached to wooden shafts and used for hunting large game. These tools were primarily used to hunt **megafauna**, which provided essential resources for survival.

The **Clovis people** had a profound relationship with the large animals that roamed the North American continent. Archaeological evidence suggests that these early humans were not only hunters of mammoths and other megafauna but also **scavengers** and **toolmakers**, using every part of the animals for food, clothing, and shelter. However, the **disappearance of megafauna** at the end of the Pleistocene had a significant impact on the **Clovis culture**.

2. The Onset of the Younger Dryas: A Climate Crisis

As the Younger Dryas event began, temperatures in the Northern Hemisphere dropped dramatically, with some regions experiencing a sudden **10°C (18°F)** temperature decrease over just a few decades. This abrupt cooling period was accompanied by a series of **environmental changes** that would have drastically affected the ecosystems in which the Clovis people lived:

- **Glacial Expansion**: The retreating ice sheets that had covered much of North America began to expand again, leading to **colder and harsher climates** in some areas.
- **Vegetation Shifts**: The cooling temperatures led to a contraction of the **temperate forests** and **grasslands**, and a rise in the coverage of **tundra-like** environments, drastically altering the availability of food and resources for both humans and animals.
- **Disruption of Ecosystems**: The ecosystems that had sustained **megafauna** and **early humans** for millennia were disrupted, with **vegetation** becoming less abundant and **water sources** drying up or shifting, creating a challenging environment for the large animals that the Clovis people depended on.

3. The Extinction of Megafauna

The megafauna of North America, which included iconic species like the **mammoth, mastodon, giant sloth,** and **saber-toothed cat**, were key components of the continent's ecosystems. These large animals were well-adapted to the cold, glacial environments of the late Pleistocene. However, by the time the Younger Dryas struck, many of these species were pushed to the brink of extinction.

The **mammoth** is one of the most iconic examples of this megafaunal collapse. These massive herbivores roamed across the **grasslands** and **tundra** of North America, feeding on grasses, shrubs, and small trees. They were well-adapted to cold environments, with long, shaggy fur, large tusks, and a unique ability to endure freezing temperatures. However, the Younger Dryas marked the beginning of the end for these creatures, as the changing climate and **reduction in available food** likely caused widespread stress and population decline.

The exact causes of the **extinction** of these megafauna are still debated, but the Younger Dryas cooling is believed to have been a significant factor. Several theories propose that the **climate shift**:

1. **Reduced Habitats**: As temperatures dropped and the climate became colder and wetter, the expansive grasslands that supported **mammoths** and other large herbivores were replaced by colder forests or tundra, reducing the available food sources.

2. **Disruption of Ecosystems**: The Younger Dryas triggered a collapse in the food web. As large herbivores like mammoths struggled to find food, the carnivores that preyed on them, like **saber-toothed cats** and **short-faced bears**, would have suffered as well.

3. **Increased Stress**: The **intensified cold** and a lack of adequate nutrition likely caused **reproductive failure** and high mortality among megafauna. For long-lived species like mammoths, this could have spelled a **rapid decline** in population numbers.

4. **Human Hunting Pressure**: While climatic factors were likely the primary cause, the Clovis people may have contributed to the **megafaunal extinctions** through **overhunting**. The **Clovis points** found at archaeological sites indicate that the Clovis people hunted these animals, which could have placed additional pressure on populations already stressed by climate change.

The **extinction** of megafauna such as mammoths and mastodons had a ripple effect on the entire ecosystem, disrupting food chains and ecological balance. It is likely that other species, like the **giant sloth**, **giant**

bison, and **camelid species**, also faced similar fates due to both climate change and human activity.

4. The Decline of the Clovis Culture

As the **megafauna** disappeared, the **Clovis culture**—which had relied heavily on large game hunting—also faced significant challenges. The **Clovis people** had specialized in hunting and processing **megafauna**, using tools like the **Clovis point** to take down large prey. With the extinction of mammoths, mastodons, and other megafauna, the Clovis people were forced to adapt their way of life.

Several changes occurred as a result:

1. **Cultural Shifts**: As large game became scarcer, the Clovis people likely had to shift their focus to smaller game such as **deer**, **bison**, and **rabbits**, or increasingly rely on **fishing** and **gathering** plant-based food. This change in subsistence strategies would have required modifications to their tools and social structures.

2. **Technological Adaptation**: While the **Clovis point** was designed for hunting large animals, it is believed that the Clovis people adapted their toolkits to hunt smaller game. Evidence of this shift can be seen in the development of **microblades** and other **specialized tools** for processing smaller prey and gathering plant material.

3. **Cultural Disintegration or Transformation**: Some researchers propose that the **extinction of megafauna** and the subsequent environmental changes contributed to the **collapse** of the Clovis culture. Without the large, predictable game populations they relied on, the Clovis people may have experienced **food shortages**, leading to social disintegration and a potential **shift** in cultural practices. Alternatively, this collapse might have spurred the rise of **new cultures** and **subsistence strategies**, such as the development of **early agricultural practices** or **regionalized hunting traditions**.

4. **Population Decline**: Archaeological evidence suggests that the Clovis population may have **declined sharply** after the megafaunal extinctions, possibly due to **food scarcity, social upheaval**, and environmental stress. This could explain why the Clovis culture disappeared so suddenly, giving way to the later **Archaic cultures** in

North America, who adapted to a changing environment and focused more on **foraging** and **hunting smaller game**.

5. The Aftermath: A New Ecosystem and Human Adaptation

By the end of the Younger Dryas, around 11,700 years ago, the Earth began warming again, marking the transition into the **Holocene** epoch. This warming led to the rise of new **ecosystems** and a complete reshaping of the environment. With the extinction of megafauna, new species of plants and animals began to dominate, and human societies, such as those in the **Archaic period**, adapted to the **new landscape**.

In response to the disappearance of large game, early humans began to focus more on **smaller game**, **plant domestication**, and **early agriculture**, setting the stage for the rise of **agricultural societies** and the eventual emergence of **complex civilizations**. These changes laid the foundation for the development of North American cultures in the millennia that followed.

The Younger Dryas period was a time of profound upheaval for the **Clovis culture** and the **megafauna** that once roamed North America. The abrupt cooling of the climate, combined with the extinction of key species and the pressure from human hunting, reshaped the continent's ecosystems and forced early human cultures to adapt. While the Clovis people were able to survive for a time by adjusting their subsistence strategies, the end of the megafauna era marked the beginning of a new chapter in both the **history of life** on Earth and the evolution of **human societies** in North America.

Part II: The Global Flood Myth Archetype

Chapter 6: The Concept of Catastrophic Floods in Mythology

Flood myths are among the most **widespread and enduring** themes in world mythology, transcending geographical, cultural, and historical boundaries. These myths, which describe vast and destructive floods that often sweep across the Earth, have been recorded in the mythologies of nearly every culture, from the ancient civilizations of Mesopotamia to the Indigenous traditions of the Americas, and from the tales of ancient Greece to the myths of the Far East. The **universal nature** of flood myths suggests that they may have originated from a shared human experience of **catastrophic flooding** or similar environmental catastrophes, potentially linked to **climate change events** such as the **Younger Dryas**.

In this chapter, we will explore the **universal presence of flood myths** in human cultures, their symbolic meanings, and the possible historical and environmental events that may have inspired these stories. We will also examine the connections between **catastrophic floods** and the Younger Dryas period, offering a glimpse into how ancient civilizations may have understood and incorporated real-world catastrophes into their mythologies.

1. The Universal Theme of Flood Myths

Flood myths appear in the traditions of cultures all over the world, even in regions that are geographically distant from one another. These myths often share common elements: a massive flood that inundates the world, a deity or divine figure who causes or oversees the flood, and a small group of survivors who endure the disaster and repopulate the Earth.

Common themes found in many flood myths include:

- **Divine Retribution**: Floods are often depicted as acts of divine wrath, sent by gods to punish humanity for its sins, moral corruption, or disobedience. The flood represents a **cleansing** or **reset** of the world, wiping away the old order and making way for a new one.

- **A Chosen Survivor**: A common feature in many flood myths is the **figure of a survivor**—usually a hero or a group of humans—who are chosen by the gods or fate to survive the deluge. These survivors often embark on a journey to repopulate the Earth and restore order.

- **The Ark or Vessel**: Many flood myths include a **vessel** or **ark** that carries the survivors to safety. This vessel is often an act of divine intervention, designed to ensure the preservation of life in the wake of the disaster.

- **Rebirth and Renewal**: After the floodwaters subside, the world is often depicted as being renewed or reborn. The survivors are tasked with the responsibility of rebuilding civilization and restoring balance to a world that has been reset by the flood.

2. Prominent Flood Myths Across Cultures

The most well-known and widely studied flood myth is the **story of Noah's Ark** in the **Bible**. However, countless other cultures have their own versions of catastrophic floods. Here are just a few examples:

- **Mesopotamian Mythology**: One of the oldest and most famous flood myths comes from **Mesopotamia**, particularly the **Epic of Gilgamesh**. In this myth, the hero **Utnapishtim** is warned by the god **Ea** of an impending flood that will destroy all life on Earth. He builds a large boat, similar to Noah's Ark, to save himself, his family, and a selection of animals. The flood is described as a divine punishment, and after it subsides, Utnapishtim's boat comes to rest on a mountain, and life is renewed.

- **Biblical Tradition**: In the Hebrew Bible, the story of **Noah's Ark** in the **Book of Genesis** describes a great flood sent by God to destroy a sinful humanity. Noah, a righteous man, is chosen to build an ark to save himself, his family, and pairs of each species of animal. The floodwaters cover the Earth, and after the waters recede, Noah's descendants repopulate the world.

- **Greek Mythology**: In Greek mythology, the flood myth is told through the story of **Deucalion and Pyrrha**. According to the myth, the Greek gods decided to flood the world to rid it of its wickedness. Deucalion and Pyrrha, warned by the Titan **Prometheus**, built a chest (or ark) to survive the flood. After the waters receded, the couple repopulated the Earth by throwing stones behind them, which transformed into humans.

- **Hindu Mythology**: The Hindu tradition contains a flood myth in the **Satapatha Brahmana**, where the god **Vishnu**, in the form of a giant fish, warns the sage **Manu** of a coming flood. Manu, with the help of Vishnu, builds a large boat that saves him, his family, and the seven sages. After the floodwaters subside, the Earth is repopulated.

- **Native American Mythology**: In the **Iroquois** tradition, there is a story of a great flood that was caused by the actions of the **Great Spirit**. The flood covered the world and only a small group of survivors, who were saved in a floating canoe, survived. Similarly, the **Ojibwe** people have a flood myth in which a great deluge destroys the Earth, and the survivors repopulate the world after the waters recede.

- **Andean Mythology**: In South American cultures, such as the **Inca** civilization, flood myths also abound. In **Inca mythology**, the first humans were created by the god **Viracocha**, and a flood was sent to destroy the corrupt world. A small group of survivors were chosen to repopulate the Earth after the floodwaters receded.

- **Australian Aboriginal Mythology**: Many Indigenous Australian cultures have flood myths. In some stories, **Rainbow Serpents** or other spirits send a flood to cleanse the world, often in response to human actions. These floods are sometimes followed by a **rebirth** of the land and its creatures.

3. The Symbolism of Flood Myths

Flood myths carry deep **symbolic significance**. While they are often rooted in specific cultural contexts, many of their themes resonate across cultures. Some of the key symbolic meanings include:

- **Purification and Renewal**: Floods are frequently symbolic of a **cleansing** or **purification** of the Earth. In many myths, the floodwaters sweep away corruption and sin, leaving behind a new world that is pure and ready for renewal. This idea of **rebirth** after destruction is a common motif, with survivors often tasked with rebuilding and repopulating the Earth.

- **Human Vulnerability and Divine Will**: Flood myths also underscore the **vulnerability of humans** in the face of natural forces. The flood is often depicted as an expression of **divine wrath** or a force of nature that humans cannot control. This reflects the belief that humans must live in accordance with divine or natural laws to avoid destruction.

- **Cyclic Time and Repetition**: Flood myths often suggest that time is cyclical and that the destruction and rebirth of the world will continue in an eternal cycle. This reflects the **repetitive nature of time** in many mythologies, where disasters are followed by renewal, and history repeats itself.

- **The Fragility of Civilization**: Many flood myths point to the fragility of human civilization. The flood, in many cases, is a reminder that human efforts to build societies and cultures are ultimately vulnerable to the whims of nature or the will of the gods.

4. The Younger Dryas and the Origin of Flood Myths

Given the global prevalence of flood myths, some researchers suggest that these stories may be linked to real **historical events**, such as **catastrophic floods** caused by the **end of the last Ice Age**. The **Younger Dryas**—an abrupt, severe climate event that caused rapid cooling and environmental upheaval around 12,800 years ago—could have been the source of many of these flood myths.

- **Glacial Lake Missoula Flood**: In North America, the **Glacial Lake Missoula Flood** is a well-documented event that occurred around 13,000 years ago, near the end of the Ice Age. A massive glacial lake in what is now Montana catastrophically released billions of tons of water, creating immense floods that swept across large portions of the Pacific Northwest. This event could have been a source of inspiration for the flood myths of **Native American cultures**.

- **Sea Level Rise**: The end of the Ice Age was also marked by the melting of glaciers, leading to a **rise in sea levels**. This gradual increase in sea levels could have caused coastal flooding and the submerging of land, creating the conditions for flood myths in ancient maritime societies, such as the **Mediterranean** and **Near East**.

- **Global Climate Events**: The cooling period of the **Younger Dryas** could have also caused abrupt shifts in weather patterns, including torrential rains and flooding, which would have been interpreted as divine or catastrophic events by early human societies. These events could have been passed down through generations as part of their mythological traditions.

Flood myths serve as a powerful reminder of the **shared human experience** with natural disasters. The common thread running through these myths suggests that, across cultures, the memory of a great flood or environmental catastrophe has been passed down for millennia. It is possible that the **Younger Dryas** climate event, with its abrupt cooling and environmental disruptions, played a role in shaping the widespread myths of catastrophic floods.

As we explore these myths in greater detail, we see how they reflect **human responses to environmental change**, and how **mythology** serves as both a record of cultural memory and an attempt to explain and make sense of **catastrophic events** that were beyond human control. The Younger Dryas may have been one such event, and its memory could have been woven into the fabric of the world's most enduring and universal flood myths.

Chapter 7: The Sumerian Flood: Gilgamesh and the Flood Tablet

The **Sumerian flood myth** is one of the oldest and most significant accounts of a great deluge, and it is primarily found in the **Epic of Gilgamesh**, one of the earliest works of literature from ancient Mesopotamia. The flood story in the Epic of Gilgamesh tells of a catastrophic flood that wiped out almost all life on Earth, a divine retribution against human wickedness. This myth is crucial not only because it is one of the most famous versions of the flood tale but also because it shares striking similarities with other ancient flood myths, such as the biblical **Noah's Ark** and the flood myths of other civilizations.

At the heart of the Sumerian version of the flood myth is the story of **Utnapishtim**, a man who is forewarned by the god **Ea** of an impending deluge, allowing him to survive and ultimately become immortal. The tale provides rich insights into **Sumerian beliefs**, their relationship with the gods, and their perceptions of **moral order** and **divine retribution**.

In this chapter, we will explore the **Sumerian flood myth**, its key characters, and its significance in the context of the broader narrative of the **Epic of Gilgamesh**. We will also examine the **Flood Tablet**—the part of the Epic of Gilgamesh that recounts the flood story—and how it links the Sumerian myth to other ancient accounts of deluges.

1. The Epic of Gilgamesh: An Introduction

The **Epic of Gilgamesh** is an ancient Sumerian epic poem that dates back to at least the **third millennium BCE**, although the most complete versions were recorded in **Akkadian** during the **Babylonian period** (around the 12th century BCE). The poem is composed of **twelve tablets** and tells the story of **Gilgamesh**, the king of Uruk, and his adventures, trials, and eventual quest for immortality.

While the narrative focuses on Gilgamesh's search for eternal life, it is also deeply concerned with themes such as the meaning of **life**, **death**, and **human suffering**. The **flood story**—which appears in Tablet XI of the epic—is a crucial part of Gilgamesh's journey. After Gilgamesh's close companion **Enkidu** dies, Gilgamesh becomes obsessed with finding a way to avoid death and live forever. His quest leads him to meet **Utnapishtim**, a character who holds the secret of immortality, and the story of Utnapishtim's survival of the great flood is central to the wisdom he imparts to Gilgamesh.

2. The Story of Utnapishtim: A Divine Warning

In the **Epic of Gilgamesh**, **Utnapishtim** is a figure who is granted immortality by the gods, a gift that is linked to his survival of a devastating flood. According to the myth, Utnapishtim was once a mortal king who lived in a city similar to the great cities of Sumer, possibly the legendary **Shuruppak**. When the gods became dissatisfied with humanity's behavior—specifically their noise, wickedness, or corruption—they decided to send a great flood to wipe out all life on Earth.

However, the god **Ea**, who was sympathetic to humans, decided to warn Utnapishtim. Ea appeared to Utnapishtim in a dream and told him that a deluge would come, but he should not fear. Instead, Utnapishtim was instructed to **build a boat** to save himself, his family, and a select group of animals from the flood.

The boat was to be made of **pitch** and **reed**, and Utnapishtim was told the exact measurements for its construction, much like the instructions given to Noah in the Bible. He was also told to **seal the boat** and ensure that it would carry enough supplies to support life during the flood's duration.

Utnapishtim obeyed the divine command and built the boat, loading it with his family, craftsmen, and the animals that Ea had instructed him to save. Once the boat was sealed, the flood began, and it raged for **seven days and seven nights**, submerging the Earth completely. The floodwaters were described as so violent that they **destroyed the Earth's surface**, and even the gods, witnessing the devastation, were filled with fear.

3. The Flood: Seven Days of Destruction

The flood itself is described in vivid detail in the **Flood Tablet**. During the seven-day deluge, **Utnapishtim's boat** floated on the waters, and the devastation was immense. The storm unleashed by the gods was said to be so catastrophic that it wiped out every living thing on the planet, including humans, animals, and plants. The text is filled with imagery of **chaos** and **destruction**, portraying the flood as a **cosmic reset**, one that symbolizes the power of the gods and their ability to completely annihilate humanity.

The narrative emphasizes the divine power behind the flood, illustrating the gods' wrath and their ability to destroy life on Earth when they deem it necessary. The gods' fear of the flood, particularly their regret over unleashing such destruction, adds a complex layer of emotional depth to the myth. Once the storm subsided, the gods were horrified to see the devastation and expressed regret for their actions, realizing the catastrophic consequences of their decisions.

4. The End of the Flood: Rebirth and Survival

After the storm finally ceased, Utnapishtim's boat came to rest on **Mount Nisir**, which is often identified with a mountain in the **Zagros range** (modern-day Iraq). Utnapishtim opened a window on the boat, and a dove was released to find dry land. The dove returned, finding no resting place, so Utnapishtim released a swallow, which also returned without a place to land. Finally, he sent out a raven, which did not return, signaling that the waters had receded and that dry land had emerged.

After the floodwaters receded, Utnapishtim offered a **sacrifice** to the gods, and the gods, in turn, rewarded him for his obedience. In recognition of Utnapishtim's survival, and as a reward for his faithfulness, the gods granted him **immortality**. He and his wife were taken to the **distant land of the gods**, where they lived forever, untouched by death.

The flood story thus serves as both a narrative of divine punishment and a tale of survival, where a righteous individual, warned by a god, survives to witness the rebirth of the world. In Utnapishtim's case, this survival also leads to the bestowal of eternal life, a reward that is offered to him as a rare and exceptional gift from the gods.

5. The Significance of the Sumerian Flood Myth

The Sumerian version of the flood story is significant for several reasons:

- **Divine Justice and Retribution**: The flood is portrayed as a form of divine justice, a means of punishing humanity for its perceived moral failings. The gods in the story are not simply vengeful, but also regretful of the destruction they caused. This reflects a complex view of the gods as both powerful and fallible, adding depth to the narrative.

- **Symbolism of Rebirth**: The flood serves as a **resetting** of the world, clearing the way for a new era. This motif of destruction leading to rebirth is common in many flood myths, symbolizing the cyclical nature of life, death, and renewal.

- **The Relationship Between Humans and Gods**: Utnapishtim's survival and subsequent immortality suggest a unique relationship between humans and gods, one that involves divine favor and intervention. The story emphasizes the **importance of obedience to the gods** and the idea that survival is often a divine gift, not a human right.

- **Connection with Other Flood Myths**: The Sumerian flood myth shares numerous similarities with other ancient flood stories, particularly the **biblical** story of Noah. Both feature a righteous individual saved from destruction, the building of a great boat, the sending out of birds to find dry land, and the promise of a new beginning after the flood. These similarities suggest a shared cultural heritage or common historical events that influenced these stories across civilizations.

6. The Flood Tablet and Its Historical Context

The **Flood Tablet**, which contains the account of the flood in the **Epic of Gilgamesh**, is an essential part of the epic and has survived in several versions. The version most commonly studied comes from the **Babylonian** text, which was recorded in **Akkadian** on twelve tablets. The Flood Tablet itself is an **important piece of literature**, and its inclusion in the Epic of Gilgamesh places the story within a broader narrative about the nature of humanity, divine intervention, and the quest for immortality.

Archaeologists and historians believe the **Flood Tablet** was based on earlier Sumerian myths, with some of its elements possibly originating from even older Mesopotamian flood stories. The Flood Tablet also contains echoes of **historical floods** that may have occurred in the region, particularly the flooding of the **Tigris and Euphrates** rivers, which would have had significant social and cultural impacts on ancient Mesopotamian civilizations.

The **Sumerian flood myth** stands as one of the earliest and most significant expressions of the flood motif in world mythology. Through the story of **Utnapishtim**, the myth captures themes of **divine justice**, **rebirth**, and **human survival** in the face of catastrophic destruction. The parallels between the Sumerian flood story and later myths, such as the biblical **Noah's Ark**, suggest that the Sumerian version of the flood has had a profound influence on subsequent religious and cultural traditions.

By exploring the **Flood Tablet** in detail, we gain valuable insight into the ancient Mesopotamian worldview, their understanding of the gods, and the role of natural disasters in shaping their myths and beliefs. The Sumerian flood myth is not just a narrative of destruction, but a story of survival, divine favor, and the renewal of life in the aftermath of catastrophe.

Chapter 8: Noah's Ark: The Biblical Flood Myth

The story of **Noah's Ark** is one of the most well-known and enduring narratives in religious and cultural history. Recorded in the **Book of**

Genesis in the **Bible**, it tells the tale of how God, dissatisfied with the wickedness of humankind, decides to send a great flood to cleanse the Earth. However, Noah, a righteous man, is chosen by God to build an ark—a giant boat—to save his family and representatives of the animal kingdom. The flood wipes out all life, but Noah and his family survive, beginning the repopulation of Earth after the waters recede.

The biblical flood narrative shares many characteristics with other ancient flood myths, including the Sumerian **Epic of Gilgamesh** and the **Greek** story of Deucalion. These similarities suggest that the flood myth may stem from common human experiences with natural disasters, such as flooding, or that these myths are reflections of shared cultural memories of cataclysmic events. In this chapter, we will delve into the details of Noah's Ark, its theological significance, and how the story compares to other flood myths from around the world.

1. The Biblical Flood Story: Noah's Ark

The flood story in the **Bible** is found primarily in **Genesis 6-9**, where it is detailed in several stages:

- **The Wickedness of Humankind**: The narrative begins with the description of humanity's moral corruption. The people of the Earth had become evil, and their violence and sin had reached a level that God could no longer tolerate. As a result, God decided to destroy all life, both human and animal, with a **great flood**.

- **God's Covenant with Noah**: Noah, however, is described as a righteous man in a world of wickedness. In **Genesis 6:9**, Noah is said to have "walked with God," implying his closeness to the divine and his adherence to God's commandments. God chooses Noah to build an ark, warning him of the coming flood and providing detailed instructions on how to construct the vessel. The ark is to be made of **cypress wood, pitch**, and it is to be large enough to house Noah's family—his wife, three sons, and their wives—as well as a pair of every kind of animal on Earth.

- **The Great Flood**: Once the ark is built, Noah and his family, along with the animals, board the ark. God causes it to rain for **forty days and forty nights**, flooding the Earth and covering even the highest mountains. All life on Earth is wiped out except for those in the ark.

This deluge is portrayed as **divine retribution** for the sins of humanity, a theme common to many flood myths.

- **The End of the Flood**: After the rain ceases, the waters remain high for a period of time. Noah releases a **raven**, which flies around but does not return, and then a **dove**, which first returns without finding dry land, and then returns with an olive leaf, signaling that the floodwaters are receding. After another period, the ark finally comes to rest on the **mountains of Ararat** (traditionally identified with a mountain range in present-day **Turkey**). The floodwaters subside, and Noah and his family exit the ark, marking the **rebirth** of the Earth.

- **God's Covenant with Noah**: After the flood, God makes a **covenant** with Noah and all living creatures, promising that He would never again destroy the Earth with a flood. As a symbol of this promise, God places the **rainbow** in the sky. This covenant ensures the continued survival of humanity and the Earth, and Noah's descendants are tasked with repopulating and stewarding the planet.

2. Theological and Moral Themes in Noah's Ark

The story of **Noah's Ark** carries significant theological and moral lessons, which are central to its role in **Judaism, Christianity**, and **Islam**:

- **Divine Judgment and Mercy**: The flood is a form of divine judgment on a corrupt humanity. God's decision to destroy the Earth, however, is tempered by His mercy in choosing Noah to survive. This duality of **justice and mercy** is a core element of the story and serves to highlight both God's power and His desire for righteousness.

- **Humanity's Sin and Redemption**: The flood is often seen as a **symbolic cleansing** of the Earth from sin. It represents the **moral decay** of humanity and the need for divine intervention to restore order. Noah's obedience to God's commands highlights the importance of faithfulness and **righteousness** in the face of overwhelming evil.

- **Covenant and Promise**: The **rainbow** serves as a symbol of God's covenant with Noah and all living creatures, a promise that God will never again destroy the Earth with a flood. This covenant represents a commitment to creation and to the ongoing relationship between humanity and God. It underscores the idea of **divine loyalty** to the Earth and to those who honor and obey God.

3. Noah's Ark and Other Flood Myths

The story of Noah's Ark bears striking similarities to other ancient flood myths from cultures around the world. These similarities suggest that the story of Noah may not be unique, but rather part of a larger tradition of flood myths that reflect common cultural experiences or collective memories of catastrophic floods. Below are some key examples of other flood myths:

- **The Sumerian Flood (Epic of Gilgamesh)**: As discussed in previous chapters, the **Sumerian** flood myth features the character **Utnapishtim**, who survives a great flood sent by the gods to punish humanity. Like Noah, Utnapishtim is warned by a god (Ea) and instructed to build a boat to save his family and a variety of animals. The flood lasts for **seven days and seven nights**, and after the waters recede, Utnapishtim is granted immortality by the gods, similar to how Noah and his family repopulate the Earth after the flood.

- **The Greek Flood (Deucalion and Pyrrha)**: In **Greek mythology**, the story of **Deucalion** and his wife **Pyrrha** parallels that of Noah. According to the myth, the gods decide to flood the Earth to punish humanity for its corruption. Deucalion, the son of the Titan **Prometheus**, is warned of the flood and instructed to build a large chest to save himself and his wife. After the floodwaters recede, the couple repopulates the Earth by throwing stones over their shoulders, which turn into humans. Similar to Noah, Deucalion and Pyrrha are depicted as the **chosen survivors** who help renew the Earth after the deluge.

- **The Hindu Flood Myth (Manu and the Fish)**: In **Hindu** mythology, the flood story centers around **Manu**, a sage who is warned by the god **Vishnu** (in the form of a giant fish) about an impending flood. Manu is instructed to build a boat and take with him the **saptarishi** (seven sages) and samples of all plant and animal life. After the flood subsides, Manu and the sages are tasked with repopulating the

Earth. This myth shares many similarities with the Noah story, including the idea of a **chosen survivor** and the **preservation of life**.

- **The Native American Flood Myths**: Various **Indigenous peoples** of North America also have their own flood stories. For example, the **Ojibwe** and **Iroquois** tribes have myths in which a great flood wipes out humanity due to its evil ways. A small group of survivors is saved in a canoe or ark-like vessel. Like Noah, these survivors often receive guidance from a divine figure and are tasked with **repopulating the Earth**.

- **The Chinese Flood Myth (Yu the Great)**: In **Chinese mythology**, the **Great Flood** is a central event in the story of **Yu the Great**, who is tasked with controlling the waters that have inundated the land. While not directly a flood myth in the same sense as Noah's, the story of **Yu** involves divine intervention to restore order to the world and involves themes of **survival** and **restoration** of civilization in the aftermath of disaster.

4. Key Similarities and Differences

While there are many common elements between the story of Noah's Ark and other flood myths, there are also key differences that reflect the unique cultural and theological frameworks of each tradition:

- **Divine Motivation**: In many myths, including Noah's Ark, the flood is a **divine punishment** for human wrongdoing. However, some cultures, such as the Sumerians and Greeks, depict the flood as a consequence of the gods' anger or capriciousness, rather than a moral judgment on humanity's sin.

- **Survivor's Role**: In most flood myths, the survivors are chosen by the gods for their **righteousness** or **divine favor**. However, the specific tasks given to the survivors vary. In Noah's case, he is chosen for his **obedience** to God's command, whereas in other myths, the survivors may receive specific instructions or powers to restore the Earth (e.g., Deucalion and Pyrrha repopulate the Earth by throwing stones).

- **The Flood's Duration**: While the **duration** of the flood varies in different traditions, a common motif is the idea of a **prolonged** deluge (often 40 days and 40 nights in the Bible, seven days in the Epic of Gilgamesh, and sometimes **seven or ten days** in other myths). The idea of a **lengthy flood** reflects the enormity and severity of the event.

- **The Rebirth of Earth**: After the flood, the world is often depicted as undergoing a process of **rebirth and renewal**, with the survivors taking the role of **repopulating** or **restoring life** to the Earth. This **restoration** reflects themes of **renewal and hope**, which are shared across flood myths.

The story of **Noah's Ark** stands as a foundational narrative not only in **Judaism, Christianity**, and **Islam** but also in the broader human cultural imagination. The themes of **divine judgment, mercy**, and the **renewal of life** after a catastrophe resonate deeply across cultures, as evidenced by the similarities between Noah's story and the flood myths of other ancient civilizations. These myths likely stem from shared human experiences with **flooding**, possibly inspired by catastrophic floods in the ancient world, such as the flooding of the **Tigris and Euphrates** rivers or the **Black Sea** deluge.

By comparing Noah's Ark with other flood myths, we gain insight into the universal nature of these stories and the profound impact that **natural disasters** have had on human storytelling and religious traditions. Whether as a symbol of divine retribution, as a tale of survival, or as a promise of **renewal**, the flood myth remains one of the most powerful and enduring motifs in world mythology.

Chapter 10: The Epic of Atrahasis: Babylonian Flood Mythology

The **Epic of Atrahasis** is a significant piece of **Babylonian** literature that provides a rich account of the flood myth from the perspective of **Mesopotamian** mythology. This story is one of the earliest surviving accounts of a divine deluge, predating many other flood narratives, including the **biblical** flood story of Noah, the **Sumerian** tale of **Utnapishtim**, and the **Greek** myth of **Deucalion**.

The epic is preserved on **Akkadian tablets** and dates back to around the **18th century BCE**, though its roots likely extend back even earlier. The story details how the gods, displeased with humanity's actions, decide to destroy humankind with a great flood. However, the gods choose one man, **Atrahasis**, to survive the catastrophe, allowing him and his family to repopulate the Earth after the waters subside.

1. The Story of Atrahasis: Summary and Structure

The **Epic of Atrahasis** is composed of several key sections, with the most notable being the creation of humanity, the **divine decision to send the flood**, and the flood itself. Here is a breakdown of the major events in the myth:

- **The Creation of Humankind**: In the beginning, the gods, led by **Anu**, the sky god, are burdened with labor. The lesser gods toil in the earth, digging canals and creating the world. Eventually, the gods decide to create **human beings** to relieve the lesser gods of their labor. The creation of humanity is achieved by mixing **clay** with the **blood of a slain god**, which is similar to other myths that associate the creation of humans with divine sacrifice. The newly created humans are placed on Earth to carry out the work that the gods no longer want to do.

- **The Overpopulation and Noise of Humankind**: As humanity multiplies, the noise from their activities becomes unbearable for the gods, particularly the god **Enlil**, who is disturbed by the constant clamor. Enlil, frustrated by the disruption, decides that humanity must be punished.

- **The First Plagues**: Before the flood, the gods send a series of **plagues** to reduce the human population. These plagues include **disease, famine**, and other catastrophes. However, despite the severity of these afflictions, humans continue to multiply and make noise, further angering the gods.

- **The Decision to Send the Flood**: Finally, after several failed attempts to reduce the human population, the god **Enlil** decides to send a great flood to wipe out humanity. This decision is made in response to the gods' frustration with the noise and behavior of humans. However, one god, **Ea** (also known as **Enki**), takes pity on humanity and warns **Atrahasis**, a wise and pious man, of the impending flood.

- **The Warning and Ark Construction**: Ea advises Atrahasis to build a large **boat** to survive the flood. Atrahasis is instructed to make the boat **waterproof** and **airtight** to ensure that he, his family, and the animals will survive. Atrahasis follows Ea's instructions and builds the boat, gathering two of every kind of animal and taking them aboard to ensure the survival of life after the flood.

- **The Great Flood**: The flood, sent by Enlil, is a cataclysmic event that lasts for **seven days and seven nights**, during which the Earth is completely submerged. The gods are horrified as they witness the destruction, but they cannot reverse the flood once it has begun. The floodwaters eventually subside, and Atrahasis' boat comes to rest on a **mountain**. Atrahasis and his passengers survive, and the world is left to repopulate.

- **The Rebirth of Humanity**: After the flood, Atrahasis and his family are the only survivors. The gods, realizing their actions have nearly wiped out humanity, decide to make an agreement to prevent future overpopulation. They introduce new rules to control the human population, such as limiting childbirth, and the gods establish measures to ensure a balance between human activity and divine control.

2. Themes and Symbolism in the Epic of Atrahasis

The **Epic of Atrahasis** shares several thematic elements with other ancient flood myths, particularly those from the **Sumerian** and **biblical** traditions. These include:

- **Divine Wrath and Justice**: The flood in the **Epic of Atrahasis** is a form of **divine retribution**. The gods, particularly Enlil, are angry at humanity for their noise, overpopulation, and behavior. The flood represents the gods' decision to correct this imbalance by wiping out humanity. This theme of divine wrath and punishment for human behavior is central to many ancient flood myths.

- **The Role of a Chosen Survivor**: Similar to the story of **Noah** in the Bible and **Utnapishtim** in the **Epic of Gilgamesh**, Atrahasis is chosen by the gods to survive the flood. He is portrayed as a pious, wise, and obedient figure who is instructed by the god **Ea** to build the ark. This **divine favor** is central to the flood myth, as Atrahasis becomes the survivor who will ensure the continuation of humanity after the deluge.

- **The Preservation of Life**: Like other flood myths, the **Epic of Atrahasis** emphasizes the preservation of life through the **ark**. Atrahasis takes two of every species onto the ark, ensuring that life on Earth can continue after the floodwaters recede. This motif of preservation of life, particularly through divine intervention, is common in many cultures' flood narratives.

- **Humanity's Role in the Cosmos**: The flood in the **Epic of Atrahasis** reflects humanity's fragile position in the divine hierarchy. The gods create humans to relieve their burden, but they also use them as instruments of divine will. The human characters in these myths are subject to the gods' actions, and their survival depends on their ability to follow divine instructions. The themes of **obedience** and **survival** under divine direction are key elements in the myth.

3. The Similarities Between the Epic of Atrahasis and Other Flood Myths

The **Epic of Atrahasis** shares a number of **key similarities** with other ancient flood stories, notably the **Sumerian** flood myth in the **Epic of Gilgamesh** and the **biblical** flood account of Noah's Ark:

- **Divine Decision to Send the Flood**: In both the **Epic of Atrahasis** and the **Epic of Gilgamesh**, the gods decide to destroy humanity because of the noise, corruption, and overpopulation of the human race. In both stories, the gods are annoyed by the disruptive behavior of humans, leading them to send a flood to cleanse the Earth.

- **The Warning and Ark Construction**: In the **Epic of Atrahasis**, the god **Ea** warns Atrahasis about the flood, just as **Enki** warns **Utnapishtim** in the **Epic of Gilgamesh**. Both figures are instructed to build an **ark** or **boat** to save their families and a selection of animals. In the **biblical** flood myth, Noah is similarly warned by God and instructed to build an ark to survive the flood.

- **The Flood's Duration**: The **Epic of Atrahasis** and the **Epic of Gilgamesh** both describe the flood as lasting for **seven days and nights**, which mirrors the **biblical** account of Noah's Ark, where it rains for forty days and forty nights. This repeated motif suggests the idea of a cataclysmic event lasting long enough to wipe out life on Earth and symbolize the seriousness of the divine judgment.

- **The Rebirth of Humanity**: After the floodwaters subside, humanity must begin again. In the **Epic of Atrahasis**, the survivors are tasked with repopulating the Earth. This theme is echoed in the **Epic of Gilgamesh** and the **biblical** flood myth, where the survivors—Utnapishtim, Noah, and their families—become the progenitors of the next generation of humanity.

- **The Role of the Gods in Reproduction**: The **Epic of Atrahasis** also introduces the concept of controlling human population growth through divine intervention. The gods decide to impose limits on human reproduction to prevent another catastrophic overpopulation. This is seen in the **biblical** flood myth as well, where God makes a covenant with Noah to control the future of humankind.

4. Key Differences in the Epic of Atrahasis

While the **Epic of Atrahasis** shares many similarities with other flood myths, there are also **distinct differences** that highlight the uniqueness of the Babylonian version:

- **Multiple Plagues Before the Flood**: In the **Epic of Atrahasis**, the gods send a series of **plagues** before deciding on the flood, including disease, famine, and drought. This sequence is not as prominent in the **Epic of Gilgamesh** or the **biblical** flood narrative, where the flood itself is the primary form of divine punishment.

- **The Role of Enlil**: In the **Epic of Atrahasis**, the god **Enlil** is the one who demands the flood as a punishment, while **Ea/Enki** is the one who intervenes to save humanity. In contrast, in the **Epic of Gilgamesh**, the gods in general, particularly **Ea**, are portrayed as more directly involved in warning Utnapishtim. In the **biblical** narrative, God alone decides to send the flood as a form of judgment.

- **Population Control**: The idea of **divine population control** in the aftermath of the flood, where humans are instructed not to multiply excessively, is a unique feature of the **Epic of Atrahasis**. This element is not present in the **biblical** or **Sumerian** versions, where the focus is more on the moral and spiritual lessons following the flood.

The **Epic of Atrahasis** represents one of the earliest and most detailed accounts of the great flood in ancient mythology. It provides insights into the **Babylonian** worldview, the relationship between humanity and the gods, and the themes of divine justice, mercy, and survival. The similarities between the **Epic of Atrahasis** and other flood myths across cultures suggest that these stories were part of a shared mythological tradition that reflected a collective memory of catastrophic events.

The **Epic of Atrahasis** continues to be a vital piece of literature for understanding the development of ancient flood myths and their cultural significance. It is a testament to the enduring human fascination with the forces of nature, the divine, and the struggle for survival in the face of overwhelming catastrophe.

Chapter 11: The Greek Flood: Deucalion and Pyrrha

The **Greek flood myth**—the story of **Deucalion** and **Pyrrha**—is one of the most iconic flood myths in Western literature and plays a significant role in understanding how ancient cultures viewed natural disasters and the divine will. The myth is recorded primarily in **Hesiod's "Works and Days"** and **Ovid's "Metamorphoses"**, both of which recount the flood as a divine punishment to cleanse the Earth. The myth's themes of survival, purification, and the repopulation of humanity offer intriguing insights into human resilience in the face of catastrophe.

1. The Myth of Deucalion and Pyrrha: A Summary

The myth of **Deucalion** and **Pyrrha** is told in several variations, but the general story is consistent across sources:

- **The Wrath of Zeus**: According to the myth, **Zeus**, the king of the Greek gods, becomes angered by the **wickedness** and **immorality** of humanity. The gods have grown tired of the sinful ways of mankind and decide to wipe out all human life on Earth through a great flood. In **Hesiod's "Works and Days"**, Zeus is described as being particularly upset by the **corruption and deceit** of mankind, which provokes the divine decision to send the flood as a punishment.

- **The Survival of Deucalion and Pyrrha**: In the myth, **Deucalion**, the son of **Prometheus**, and his wife **Pyrrha**, the daughter of **Epimetheus**, are the only survivors of the flood. Prometheus, foreseeing the deluge, had warned his son Deucalion and advised him to build an ark. Deucalion and Pyrrha take refuge in the ark, which saves them from the rising waters.

- **The Rebirth of Humanity**: After the floodwaters subside, Deucalion and Pyrrha land on a mountain, often identified as **Mount Parnassus**. They pray to the gods for help in repopulating the Earth, and the oracle of **Themis** advises them to throw the "bones of their mother" behind them. Interpreting this as a command to throw stones, Deucalion and Pyrrha do so, and the stones they cast turn into people—Deucalion's stones become men, and Pyrrha's become women. In this way, humanity is reborn, and the Earth is repopulated.

- **The Moral and Symbolism**: The story of **Deucalion and Pyrrha** has deep moral and symbolic layers. It reflects the theme of **purification through destruction**—the flood is not just a punishment, but also a means of renewing and cleansing the Earth. The rebirth of humanity through the casting of stones represents a new beginning, a fresh start for a more virtuous human race.

2. Themes and Symbolism in the Greek Flood Myth

- **Divine Wrath and Human Morality**: The Greek flood myth, like many others, centers around the **idea of divine wrath** as a response to human moral failings. In this case, humanity's wickedness leads to a cleansing flood. This theme of divine retribution is central to many ancient cultures, where natural disasters are often seen as punishment for human transgressions. The Greek flood myth, however, also introduces the possibility of redemption and renewal, with Deucalion and Pyrrha acting as the moral survivors of a devastated world.

- **Survival and Repopulation**: The survival of **Deucalion** and **Pyrrha** is symbolic of hope and continuity even after catastrophic events. Their survival, and the miraculous rebirth of humanity through the casting of stones, emphasizes the idea that life, even after destruction, can regenerate and thrive. The flood story in Greek mythology highlights the cyclical nature of life, death, and rebirth.

- **The Role of the Gods**: The gods in the Greek flood myth, particularly **Zeus**, are depicted as having both the power to destroy and to create. Zeus' decision to send the flood represents both his wrath and his ability to purify and renew the world. However, his decision to spare Deucalion and Pyrrha also shows the gods' capacity for mercy and hope for the future.

3. The Historical and Geological Context of the Greek Flood Myth

While the **Greek flood myth** is often interpreted as a work of mythology or allegory, scholars have suggested that it may have historical roots tied to **real-world events**. Many of the flood myths across the world, including that of **Deucalion and Pyrrha**, may be connected to actual cataclysmic events, particularly those that occurred during the **Younger Dryas** period, the sudden and severe climate event that took place approximately **12,000 years ago**.

- **The Younger Dryas Event**: The Younger Dryas was a period of abrupt **climate cooling** that occurred at the end of the **Pleistocene** Ice Age, leading to a drastic change in global temperatures. This sudden shift in climate could have caused **catastrophic flooding** in many regions, particularly in areas where ice sheets or glaciers were present. As the glaciers melted, enormous volumes of water would have been released into the seas, leading to rising sea levels, flooding, and the displacement of early human populations.

- **The Black Sea Deluge Hypothesis**: One possible historical origin for the Greek flood myth is the theory known as the **Black Sea deluge hypothesis**. This hypothesis posits that around 12,000 years ago, the rising **Mediterranean Sea** breached the **Bosporus Strait**, flooding the previously freshwater **Black Sea** and transforming it into the saline body of water we see today. The floodwaters would have inundated the coastal areas, displacing prehistoric human populations and leaving a lasting memory of the event in the form of flood myths.

- According to this hypothesis, the ancient Greeks, as well as other cultures, may have passed down the memory of a catastrophic flood that reshaped their world. The flooding of the **Black Sea** could have been a major event that formed the basis for flood myths in surrounding cultures, including the Greeks. The myth of **Deucalion and Pyrrha** may therefore reflect this **historical event**, with the idea of a great flood cleansing the Earth coming from collective memories of widespread flooding in the ancient world.

- **Global Flood Myths**: The flood myth of **Deucalion and Pyrrha** shares similarities with other flood myths from around the world, including the **Sumerian** and **Babylonian** flood stories, the **Noah's Ark** myth in the Bible, and the **Epic of Gilgamesh**. Many of these myths likely have a **common origin** in ancient memories of catastrophic floods caused by climate changes, such as those that occurred during the end of the last Ice Age. The **Younger Dryas** and subsequent changes in global sea levels may explain why so many ancient cultures have stories of a great flood that destroyed the world.

4. The Geological Evidence of Floods in Ancient Greece

The geography of **Greece** and its surrounding regions also supports the theory that the **Greek flood myth** could have been inspired by real-world flooding events:

- **Rising Sea Levels**: Following the end of the **Ice Age, sea levels** rose significantly due to the melting of glaciers. In the Greek world, this would have had significant effects on coastal settlements. For instance, the **Aegean Sea**, the region where Greek civilization developed, is known for its complex coastline, which could have been altered by rising sea levels and sudden floods, leading to the destruction of ancient settlements and the creation of myths to explain such catastrophes.

- **Ancient Flooded Settlements**: Archaeological evidence suggests that ancient settlements along the coastlines of the **Aegean Sea** were abandoned and flooded, particularly around the time of the Younger Dryas. Some scholars argue that these flooding events were seared into the cultural memory of these populations and were passed down through oral tradition, eventually becoming the foundation for flood myths like that of Deucalion and Pyrrha.

The **Greek flood myth** of **Deucalion and Pyrrha** stands as one of the most enduring and influential flood stories in Western mythology. It reflects deep themes of divine judgment, human survival, and the renewal of life after catastrophe. Its connection to the **Younger Dryas** and the possibility of real historical events behind the myth offer a fascinating lens through which to view ancient Greek storytelling.

As with many other flood myths around the world, the Greek story of Deucalion and Pyrrha serves as both a moral lesson and a cultural memory of a time when the Earth was changed forever by natural forces. Whether the flood of Deucalion was inspired by a real historical event or emerged purely from the realm of myth, it remains a powerful symbol of human resilience and the ability to survive and rebuild after even the most devastating of cataclysms.

Part III: A World Engulfed by Water

Chapter 12: Flood Myths in Ancient Egypt

Flood myths are not exclusive to Mesopotamian and Greco-Roman cultures, as even in **Ancient Egypt**, the concept of a great flood plays a significant role in both mythology and the understanding of natural events. Egyptian flood myths are intricately tied to the cycles of the **Nile River**, which was central to the survival and prosperity of ancient Egyptian society. These myths are not only expressions of divine powers and cosmic forces but also serve as allegories for the cyclical nature of life, death, and rebirth. In this chapter, we will explore how floods were interpreted in ancient Egyptian culture, focusing on the myth of **Osiris** and the **Nile's inundation**.

1. The Role of the Nile River in Egyptian Life

The **Nile River** was the lifeblood of Egypt, flooding annually in a cycle that brought rich soil and water to the parched land. This flood, known as the **Inundation**, occurred each year during the summer months when the **Nile's waters** rose to great heights, submerging the banks and revitalizing the soil. This annual flooding provided the fertile grounds necessary for agriculture, which was essential for the survival of Egyptian society. The **Inundation** was not only a natural phenomenon but also a **divine act**, representing the gods' role in maintaining the cosmic order.

- **Divine Connection**: The Egyptians believed that the **Nile flood** was a gift from the gods, an act of divine mercy and blessing. The floodwaters were seen as a manifestation of the gods' power, bringing **fertility**, **life**, and **renewal** to the land. The flooding was crucial for Egypt's agriculture, providing the necessary conditions for growing crops and sustaining life. As a result, the **Nile flood** was celebrated with festivals and rituals, particularly in honor of the god **Hapi**, the god of the Nile, who was believed to bring the inundation.

2. The Myth of Osiris and the Nile's Inundation

While the flooding of the Nile was a natural event, **Egyptian mythology** imbued this phenomenon with deep symbolic meaning. The most important flood-related myth in Egyptian culture involves **Osiris**, the god of agriculture, life, death, and rebirth, and the **inundation of the Nile**.

The Story of Osiris and His Death

The myth of **Osiris** is one of the most significant and widely known stories in Egyptian religion and ties directly to the **annual flooding of the Nile**. The myth is rooted in the **cosmic struggle between good and evil**, between order and chaos, and between life and death.

- **Osiris** is originally depicted as a benevolent ruler, the god of agriculture, and the provider of fertility to Egypt. His reign is associated with abundance and prosperity, much like the nurturing effects of the Nile flood on the land. However, Osiris's younger brother, **Set**, the god of chaos, desert, and storms, grows jealous of Osiris's popularity and power.

- **Set's Plot Against Osiris**: Set devises a plan to murder Osiris and take his throne. He tricks Osiris into lying down in a beautifully decorated coffin, which he then seals and throws into the Nile. The coffin, carrying the body of Osiris, is swept away by the river, and eventually, it is carried to **Byblos** (a city in Phoenicia), where it becomes embedded in the trunk of a tree. Osiris's wife, **Isis**, mourns her husband's death and embarks on a search to retrieve his body.

- **The Resurrection of Osiris**: Eventually, Isis finds the body of Osiris and, using her magical powers, brings him back to life long enough to conceive their son, **Horus**. However, Osiris cannot remain in the world of the living. He descends to the **underworld**, where he becomes the ruler of the afterlife, overseeing the judgment of the dead.

The Inundation as a Symbol of Osiris's Death and Resurrection

The myth of Osiris reflects **death and rebirth**, and it was deeply linked to the **Nile flood**. The **flooding of the Nile** symbolized the death and resurrection of Osiris each year, as the river's rise and fall mirrored the cyclical nature of Osiris's life.

- **Osiris's Body and the Nile**: In one interpretation of the myth, Osiris's body is associated with the waters of the Nile. The annual flood represents the **death of Osiris**, where his body is taken into the river, symbolizing the temporary disappearance of life. Just as Osiris dies, the land of Egypt would appear to "die" as it is submerged under floodwaters.

- **The Resurrection of the Land**: The return of the waters to the land of Egypt was not only a symbol of the physical nourishment of the earth but also a reflection of Osiris's **resurrection**. After the floodwaters recede, the land is renewed, and agriculture flourishes, symbolizing the return of life from death. This represents the cyclical nature of Osiris's reign: his death marks the end of the old year, and his resurrection heralds the beginning of the new cycle.

- **Osiris as the Nile**: In the myth, Osiris is often identified with the **Nile River** itself. His very essence is intertwined with the life-giving waters of the Nile. The flood, therefore, is not only a natural event but a cosmic ritual that mirrors the death and rebirth of the god. Just as Osiris brings fertility and life to the land, so too does the inundation of the Nile provide the necessary elements for agricultural prosperity.

3. Symbolism of the Nile Flood and Osiris's Myth

The flood myth surrounding **Osiris** is filled with rich symbolism that ties together the natural world with the divine order:

- **Death and Renewal**: The myth underscores the theme of **life after death**, and the Nile flood serves as a powerful metaphor for this eternal cycle. Just as Osiris is reborn each year through the floodwaters, the land itself is reborn, rejuvenated, and made fertile. The myth encourages a view of the natural world as one that is constantly renewing itself, with destruction always followed by creation.

- **Fertility and Agriculture**: The central role of **agriculture** in the myth ties Osiris directly to the well-being of the Egyptian people. As the god of agriculture and fertility, Osiris's death and resurrection correspond to the cycles of planting and harvest. The Nile's floodwaters bring the nutrients needed for crops to grow, just as Osiris's resurrection is seen as essential for the prosperity and growth of Egyptian society.

- **Cosmic Order (Maat)**: The myth also reflects the Egyptian concept of **Maat**—the idea of cosmic order, justice, and balance. The flood and subsequent return of life align with the principle of Maat, as the gods are believed to restore balance and harmony to the world. Osiris's death and rebirth ensure that the world remains in balance, with life continually cycling between death and renewal, in a perpetual harmony that mirrors the cyclical nature of the Nile's flood.

4. Other Flood Myths in Ancient Egypt

While the myth of Osiris is the most famous Egyptian flood myth, there are other accounts and ideas related to flooding in Egyptian mythology. The annual inundation of the Nile was also linked to various gods, including **Hapi**, the god of the Nile who was often depicted as a man with a large belly and the **ankhs** (symbols of life) in his hands. The Egyptians saw **Hapi** as the embodiment of the river's fertility and abundance, and rituals were held in his honor to ensure the success of the Nile's flooding.

Some texts, such as the **Coffin Texts** and the **Pyramid Texts**, reference great floods that may have been based on earlier cultural memories of catastrophic events, potentially tying in with the **Younger Dryas** impact and the changes to global climate that resulted in catastrophic floods in many regions. The focus of Egyptian flood myths, however, is mostly centered around the cycle of the **Nile's inundation** and the divine relationship between the gods and the river.

5. The Historical and Geological Context: The Younger Dryas and Egyptian Flood Myths

The Egyptian flood myth, particularly the story of **Osiris**, may have origins tied to the ancient floods associated with the end of the **Ice Age** and the onset of the **Holocene** epoch. While the Nile's seasonal flooding was primarily an annual event caused by the monsoon rains and snowmelt in the Ethiopian Highlands, it is possible that earlier **cataclysmic floods** (such as those caused by the melting of glaciers during the end of the **Younger Dryas**) might have influenced the flood myths.

Some scholars suggest that the **global cooling** of the Younger Dryas period could have had significant effects on **North Africa**, potentially altering the flow and magnitude of rivers such as the Nile. These early and potentially catastrophic floods could have left a lasting cultural memory, which was then incorporated into Egyptian mythological narratives, particularly those revolving around **death**, **rebirth**, and the cyclical nature of life and death.

Flood myths in **Ancient Egypt**, particularly those associated with **Osiris**, underscore the deeply ingrained connection between the divine and the natural world. These myths represent the cyclical and transformative nature of life on Earth, with the **Nile's inundation** symbolizing the perpetual death and rebirth of the land and its people. The Egyptian flood myths not only explain the physical flooding of the Nile but also encapsulate a broader cosmological view of **life, death, and renewal**, and the role of the gods in maintaining cosmic balance.

As with other ancient civilizations, the flood myths of Egypt reveal a cultural effort to explain and make sense of the natural world's most powerful and unpredictable forces—floods—by embedding them in the larger narrative of divine action and cosmic order. These myths continue to offer valuable insight into the ways that ancient Egyptians viewed their world and their relationship to the forces of nature that both nurtured and threatened their existence.

Chapter 13: Flood Myths in the Americas: The Mayan and Native American Legends

Flood myths are a common theme across many ancient cultures, and the indigenous peoples of the **Americas** are no exception. Flood narratives in the Americas often carry significant cultural, spiritual, and cosmological meaning, linking humanity's survival with the forces of nature, divine intervention, and the cyclical nature of life and death. This chapter will explore the flood myths of the **Mayan civilization** and the **Native American tribes**, focusing on the **Hopi** and **Zuni** tribes, both of which offer unique insights into the role of floods in shaping their understanding of the world.

1. The Mayan Flood Myth: The Popol Vuh

The **Maya civilization**, which thrived in Mesoamerica for over a thousand years, has one of the most well-known flood myths preserved in the **Popol Vuh**, the sacred text of the **K'iche' Maya** people from present-day Guatemala. The Popol Vuh is a rich tapestry of creation myths, heroic epics, and cosmological narratives, and it includes a flood story that echoes themes found in other cultures' flood myths, such as divine punishment, the destruction of humanity, and the rebirth of life.

The Creation of Humanity and the First Flood

- **The Creation of the Earth**: In the beginning, according to the **Popol Vuh**, the Earth was covered with water, and there was no life. The gods, known as the **Heart of Sky** (or **Tepeu Kan**), decided to create the Earth, which they shaped, adding mountains, rivers, and other landforms. The gods then created plants and animals, but these creatures could not praise or worship them.

- **The Creation of Humans**: The gods tried several times to create beings who could praise them. First, they created animals, but the animals lacked intelligence and could not speak. Then, they created humans from mud, but these figures were weak and crumbled. Next, they made humans from wood, but these wooden people were soulless and unable to recognize their creators. As a result, the gods destroyed the wooden people in a great flood.

- **The Great Flood**: The gods, dissatisfied with their earlier creations, decided to send a flood to wipe out the wooden humans. In the myth, this flood comes as a **divine punishment**, cleansing the Earth of the imperfect creations. The flood represents a **recalibration of humanity**, where the gods seek to create a race of people who could properly worship and acknowledge them.

- **Survival of the Hero Twins**: Despite the destruction of the wooden people, the myth's central figures, the **Hero Twins** (known as **Hunahpu** and **Xbalanque**), survive through a series of trials and adventures. They are often seen as representing the forces of life, death, and rebirth. Following the flood and destruction of the previous generation, these twins would go on to restore order in the world.

Themes and Symbolism of the Mayan Flood Myth

- **Divine Retribution and Renewal**: Much like in other flood myths, the Mayan flood narrative reflects themes of divine retribution and renewal. The first humans, created from wood, were flawed and lacked the ability to honor the gods, so they were destroyed by a cleansing flood. The new, more refined humans—those created from maize (corn)—become the worthy descendants of the gods and play a central role in the Mayan creation story.

- **The Cycle of Life**: The flood myth in the **Popol Vuh** also represents the cyclical nature of life and death. Humanity's destruction by flood is not the end but a prelude to a new cycle of life, rebirth, and renewal. The Hero Twins are emblematic of this constant cycle of destruction and creation, where life is perpetually renewed in a cosmic rhythm.

- **Symbolism of Water**: Water in the **Mayan worldview** often symbolizes both creation and destruction. The floodwaters bring an end to the failures of the wooden people but also make way for the creation of a new, more harmonious existence. The flood cleanses the Earth, washing away the old and giving rise to the new.

2. Native American Flood Myths: The Hopi and Zuni Tribes

Native American cultures possess a wealth of rich oral traditions that include **flood myths** as foundational narratives that explain the origins of the world, humanity, and the relationship between people and nature. Among these stories, the **Hopi** and **Zuni** tribes from the **Southwestern United States** have particularly vivid and influential flood myths that reflect the interaction of spiritual forces, divine judgment, and survival.

The Hopi Flood Myth: The Great Purification

The **Hopi** people, known for their deep spiritual connection to the land and their complex religious practices, have a flood myth that centers around the idea of a **Great Purification**. This purification is a divine event, where the world is cleansed of evil and the faithful are rewarded.

- **The Emergence of Humanity**: According to the Hopi creation story, the first people emerged from the underworld, where they lived in a peaceful and prosperous world. However, as they moved into the upper world, they began to fall into corruption and sin. In response to this corruption, the **Kachina spirits** (spiritual beings who guide and protect the Hopi) warned the people of an impending catastrophe.

- **The Flood as Purification**: The Hopi believed that the flood was sent by the **Creator** to purify the world and rid it of the evil and immorality that had emerged among the people. The flood came as a form of divine judgment, and only those who had followed the teachings of the Creator and the Kachinas would survive.

- **Survival of the Chosen People**: The survivors of the Hopi flood were said to have been instructed by the Kachinas to build a **boat** or **ark**, which allowed them to endure the deluge. These survivors eventually repopulated the Earth, and the world was restored to its natural balance, with peace and harmony once again reigning.

Themes in the Hopi Flood Myth

- **Divine Judgment and Purification**: Similar to many other flood myths, the **Hopi flood myth** revolves around themes of **divine judgment** and **moral purification**. The flood is seen as a cleansing force that wipes away corruption and evil, making way for a new, morally pure world.

- **The Role of Spiritual Guides**: The **Kachina spirits** play an important role in guiding the Hopi people through the flood and ensuring their survival. These spirits are seen as the intermediaries between the people and the Creator, providing wisdom, protection, and guidance.

- **Cyclical Time and Renewal**: The Hopi people view time as cyclical, and the flood myth emphasizes the **repetition of cycles**—the destruction of the corrupt world, the survival of the righteous, and the renewal of the world.

The Zuni Flood Myth: The Story of the Bluebird and the Great Flood

The **Zuni** people, another native group from the Southwestern United States, also have a flood myth, which bears striking similarities to the Hopi story, though with distinct cultural differences.

- **The Zuni Creation Story**: According to Zuni mythology, the **first humans** lived in an earlier world, which was destroyed by a great flood. Before the flood, the world was in a state of disarray, with **chaos** and **immorality** reigning. The **gods** recognized the need for a new, purified world and sent a **Bluebird** to warn the people.

- **The Great Flood**: In the Zuni story, the flood comes as a **punishment** for the people's disregard of the gods' instructions. The floodwaters rise to cover the Earth, and only a handful of survivors, who have heeded the warning, are saved by climbing to higher ground or escaping through hidden paths.

- **Repopulation of the Earth**: After the floodwaters recede, the survivors are tasked with repopulating the Earth and restoring order to the world. The Zuni people, like the Hopi, believe that the flood was a necessary event to **purify** the world and make it a place for righteousness and balance.

Themes in the Zuni Flood Myth

- **Punishment and Cleansing**: The Zuni flood myth, like the Hopi's, emphasizes the **destructive force of water** as a divine means of punishment and purification. The flood is not just an act of nature but a spiritual cleansing, removing the impure and leaving behind a purified world.

- **Cosmic Order and Balance**: For the Zuni, the flood serves as an act of divine intervention that restores **cosmic balance**. The survivors are seen as the caretakers of this newly balanced world, tasked with ensuring harmony between the Earth, the people, and the gods.

3. Similarities Between Mayan and Native American Flood Myths

The **Mayan**, **Hopi**, and **Zuni** flood myths share several key themes:

- **Divine Judgment and Purification**: Across these myths, the flood is often a means of cleansing the world of corruption, immorality, and evil. It serves as a divine **punishment** and purification, preparing the Earth for the next phase of existence.

- **Survival and Rebirth**: In most of these flood stories, a few survivors are chosen or saved, often because of their moral integrity or adherence to divine instructions. These survivors go on to repopulate the Earth, symbolizing **rebirth** and **renewal**.

- **The Role of Water**: Water in these flood myths represents both **destruction** and **renewal**. It is a force of nature that can obliterate life but also make way for the regeneration of the world.

- **Cyclical Nature**: Many of these cultures believed in the cyclical nature of time, where death and destruction were followed by rebirth and renewal. Flood myths often reflect this worldview, with each cycle leading to a new beginning.

Flood myths in the **Americas**, particularly in **Mayan**, **Hopi**, and **Zuni** cultures, reflect the deep spiritual and cosmological understanding these societies had of the natural world. These myths symbolize the **destructive power of water**, the need for **moral integrity**, and the **cyclical nature of life and death**. By examining these flood myths, we gain insight into how ancient peoples understood their relationship with the divine, the environment, and the forces that shaped their lives.

These myths continue to resonate with modern audiences because they speak to universal themes of survival, moral renewal, and the need to live in harmony with nature. In the context of the **Younger Dryas Impact**, these flood myths may also serve as **cultural memories** of a great cataclysmic event that shaped the mythologies of the ancient world.

Chapter 15: Asian Flood Myths: The Chinese and Hindu Perspectives

Flood myths in **Asia** play a crucial role in both **Chinese** and **Hindu** cultures, and they share several similarities with other ancient flood stories around the world. These myths are not only foundational for understanding the early cosmologies and moral teachings of these civilizations but also reflect broader themes of cosmic order, divine intervention, and the restoration of balance following a cataclysmic event. In particular, the **Chinese** story of **Yu the Great** and the **Hindu** tale of **Manu** serve as central flood myths in their respective cultures. Both stories also suggest the possibility of a historical or symbolic link to ancient global catastrophes such as the end of the **Ice Age** or the **Younger Dryas** period.

1. Chinese Flood Myth: Yu the Great and the Great Flood

The **Chinese flood myth**, centered around **Yu the Great**, is one of the most significant and enduring narratives in Chinese culture. The myth dates back to ancient times and is preserved in the **Shiji** (Records of the Grand Historian) and the **Classic of Mountains and Seas**, two key historical texts. The story not only explains the origin of Chinese civilization but also reflects themes of **human perseverance**, **divine intervention**, and the importance of maintaining cosmic order.

The Great Flood and the Reign of Emperor Yao

- **The Rise of the Flood**: According to the myth, a massive and uncontrollable flood ravaged the land of **China**, threatening the very existence of its people. The floodwaters overwhelmed villages, destroyed crops, and displaced large populations. The flood lasted for many years, and despite numerous attempts to control it, the waters continued to spread, causing devastation across the land.

- **The Emperor's Mandate**: The flood, seen as a cosmic disorder, was viewed as a challenge to the balance of nature and the moral integrity of society. **Emperor Yao**, one of the legendary ancient rulers, called upon **Yu the Great**, a skilled and capable individual, to solve the problem. Yao's assignment was not only to stop the flooding but also to restore order to the world and to establish a lasting solution that would prevent further catastrophes.

- **Yu's Struggle**: Yu the Great is remembered for his tireless efforts to control the floodwaters. According to the myth, instead of merely building dams or trying to contain the water, Yu took a more **strategic approach** by **diverting** the floodwaters into channels and basins, thus draining the water back into the seas and rivers. This required years of hard labor and constant attention, as Yu worked day and night, often at great personal cost, including the separation from his family for many years.

- **Yu's Success**: After many years, Yu succeeded in managing the floodwaters, bringing peace and stability back to the land. His ability to **tame the natural world** through perseverance, wisdom, and careful planning made him a hero and a legendary figure. His success in overcoming the flood also marked his rise to power as the first ruler of the **Xia Dynasty**, making him one of the earliest emperors in Chinese history.

Themes and Symbolism in the Chinese Flood Myth

- **Restoration of Cosmic Order**: Like many flood myths, the Chinese tale of **Yu the Great** centers on the restoration of order from chaos.

The flood itself represents a natural **disorder**, and Yu's role in managing the floodwaters symbolizes the necessary human effort to bring the world back into balance, aligning with cosmic harmony.

- **Human Ingenuity and Perseverance**: Yu's success is a testament to the Chinese ideal of human **ingenuity** and **perseverance** in the face of overwhelming odds. Unlike other flood myths, which often focus on divine punishment or retribution, the Chinese story emphasizes human **resourcefulness** in overcoming nature's challenges.

- **Connection to Natural Disasters**: The flood, in Chinese mythology, is not simply an allegorical story but can also be interpreted as a metaphor for real-life events such as periodic floods or changing river systems in ancient China. These events may have been seen as **punishments from the heavens** or tests of human resilience, suggesting that ancient floods may have had a historical basis.

Yu as a Historical Figure

While **Yu the Great** is often considered a mythological figure, historical evidence suggests that his existence may have been rooted in actual events. Some scholars believe that Yu's efforts to control the Yellow River flood might have been inspired by real, large-scale flood management projects in ancient China. The figure of Yu could therefore be a symbolic representation of **human triumph** over nature's challenges, a theme echoed in flood myths worldwide.

2. Hindu Flood Myth: Manu and the Great Deluge

In **Hindu** mythology, the story of **Manu** and the **Great Flood** is one of the most important and enduring flood myths. It appears in several texts, including the **Mahabharata**, the **Ramayana**, and the **Bhagavata Purana**. The tale of Manu mirrors many other flood myths in terms of its themes of divine intervention, human survival, and the restoration of order in the world after a cataclysm.

The Warning of the Great Flood

- **The Divine Warning**: In the **Hindu flood myth**, **Manu**, the first human and a revered sage, is warned by the god **Vishnu** of an impending flood that would wipe out all life on Earth. Vishnu, in the form of a **fish**, appears to Manu, advising him to build a boat to survive the coming deluge. The fish also instructs Manu to bring the **seven sages** (or **Rishis**) and the **seeds of all plants** and **animals** with him, ensuring that life will continue after the floodwaters recede.

- **The Great Deluge**: As prophesied, the flood comes and covers the Earth, destroying all life. The floodwaters are associated with the destruction of the old world and the **purification** of the Earth. After the floodwaters subside, Manu's boat comes to rest on a **mountain**, and life begins anew, symbolizing the cycle of destruction and rebirth that is central to Hindu cosmology.

The Themes in the Hindu Flood Myth

- **Divine Intervention**: Similar to the **Yu the Great** myth in China, the flood in the **Hindu myth** is not a natural disaster that occurs randomly but is a **divine act** meant to purify and restore the world. **Vishnu**, as the protector and preserver of the universe, intervenes in human affairs to ensure that life continues after the flood.

- **The Role of Manu**: Manu's survival represents the continuation of humanity. He is often seen as the ancestor of all human beings, and his role in saving the sacred knowledge and life forms is symbolic of the **renewal** of the human race and the Earth's ecosystems.

- **The Cycle of Creation and Destruction**: The flood myth reflects Hindu beliefs in **cyclical time**—the concept that the universe goes through endless cycles of creation, destruction, and rebirth. The deluge is a powerful symbol of this process, and the survival of Manu and the sages signifies the continuation of life and wisdom after the destruction.

- **Moral and Spiritual Lessons**: In addition to its cosmological significance, the Hindu flood myth also carries moral and spiritual lessons about **obedience to divine will, humility,** and **human responsibility** for the world around them. Manu's obedience to Vishnu's command ensures his survival and the survival of life on Earth.

Comparison with Other Flood Myths

The **Hindu** and **Chinese** flood myths share many common features with other ancient flood stories, such as **divine warning**, the need for **survival**

preparation, and the restoration of **cosmic order** after a disaster. Both stories emphasize the role of a **heroic figure** (Yu in China, Manu in India) in overcoming the flood and restoring balance. Additionally, both myths also have elements of **moral purification**, where the flood serves as a means of ridding the world of corruption, immorality, or chaos.

3. Connecting the Flood Myths to Global Catastrophe

The flood myths of **China** and **India**, like those in **Mesopotamia**, **Mesoamerica**, and other parts of the world, may represent **collective memories** of a large-scale catastrophic event, such as a massive **flood** or **climatic disruption**. Some scholars have suggested that these myths could be connected to the **end of the last Ice Age** and events like the **Younger Dryas**, which were characterized by abrupt climate shifts and large-scale environmental changes that could have triggered global flooding, mass extinctions, and the upheaval of ancient civilizations.

- **Global Flood as a Cultural Memory**: The widespread nature of flood myths around the world suggests that they may be based on shared **cultural memories** of actual cataclysmic events that occurred thousands of years ago. These events could have been caused by rising sea levels, melting glaciers, or other environmental disruptions that affected large portions of the Earth's population.

- **Shared Themes of Survival and Renewal**: The consistent themes of **survival, divine intervention**, and **rebirth** in flood myths indicate that these cultures, regardless of geographic location, shared a common understanding of the cyclical nature of life and the importance of **human resilience** in overcoming great challenges.

The flood myths of **China** and **India** serve as powerful reminders of the importance of **cosmic balance, divine intervention**, and the **enduring resilience of humanity**. By comparing the flood myths of these cultures, we can better understand how ancient peoples across the world made sense of large-scale cataclysms, such as the end of the Ice Age, and how they used storytelling to explain their world's origins and their place within it. These myths offer valuable insights into the collective psyche of ancient civilizations and their attempts to comprehend and survive global catastrophes.

Chapter 17: The Flood Myths of the Pacific Islands

The Pacific Islands are home to a diverse array of cultures, each with unique traditions, languages, and mythologies. Among these, **flood myths** play a significant role in the oral traditions of many island cultures, including the **Māori** of New Zealand and the **Hawaiian** people. These myths not only reflect the deep spiritual connections these cultures have with their environments but also convey shared themes of **catastrophic events**, **divine intervention**, and the **rebirth of life** following destructive floods. By examining these flood myths, we can gain a deeper understanding of how the people of the Pacific Islands may have interpreted global catastrophes, such as **climate shifts** and **rising sea levels**, which could have shaped their cultural memories.

1. Polynesian Flood Myths: The Māori and Hawaiian Perspectives

Flood myths are a common motif in many **Polynesian cultures**, where they are often tied to natural disasters, such as **tsunamis, rising sea levels**, and other catastrophic events. The flood myths of the **Māori** and **Hawaiian** cultures share many similarities with other global flood narratives, such as those in the **Middle East**, **China**, and **India**, offering further evidence that these myths may reflect **shared experiences** of ancient global catastrophes.

The Māori Flood Myth: The Story of Tū and the Great Deluge

The **Māori** people of **New Zealand** have a rich oral tradition that includes numerous creation myths, genealogies, and stories of divine intervention. One of the most important flood myths in Māori culture is tied to the story of the great deluge, where the world is submerged by a massive flood.

- **The Flood of Tāwhirimātea**: In Māori mythology, the great flood is often associated with the deity **Tāwhirimātea**, the god of the winds and storms. Tāwhirimātea becomes enraged after the separation of the sky and the earth, a moment when the world is divided into the realms of the gods, the humans, and the natural forces. This separation causes great conflict between Tāwhirimātea and his family, including his sibling **Tāne Mahuta** (the god of forests and birds) and **Tangaroa** (the god of the sea).

- **The Deluge**: According to the myth, the anger of **Tāwhirimātea** leads to a **great flood**, as the seas rise and the waters cover the land. This catastrophic event is said to have been sent to punish humanity for the actions of the gods, and it symbolizes a cosmic **reset**, destroying the old world to make way for a new one.

- **Survival and Rebirth**: Similar to other global flood myths, the Māori narrative includes the theme of survival amidst the disaster. The survivors of the flood were said to have taken refuge in the highest mountains, such as **Maungatua**, where they waited for the waters to recede. The flood is ultimately seen as a necessary event for the purification of the world, clearing the earth of corruption and setting the stage for **renewal**. It is also interpreted as a representation of the **cosmic battle** between order and chaos, with the flood symbolizing the consequences of unchecked destruction in the world.

Themes and Symbolism in Māori Flood Myth

- **Divine Wrath and Balance**: The Māori flood myth reflects the theme of **cosmic balance** between the natural world and the gods. Tāwhirimātea's flood represents the destructive power of nature when harmony is broken between the elements. This reflects the Māori worldview of the interconnectedness of all things, including the natural environment, the gods, and humanity.

- **Moral and Spiritual Lessons**: Like other flood myths, the Māori version carries moral lessons about the consequences of human actions. The flood is seen as a form of **divine punishment**, but also as a means to cleanse and purify the world. The survivors, who are often believed to be divinely chosen, represent a **new beginning** for humanity and the possibility of **moral and spiritual renewal**.

- **Connection to Natural Disasters**: The Māori story of the flood may also be based on real-world events, such as **tsunamis**, **earthquakes**, and **flooding** caused by natural disasters. These events, which were historically significant in the Pacific region, may have influenced the development of the flood myth as a way to explain and understand such destructive occurrences.

2. Hawaiian Flood Myth: The Story of Nu'u and the Great Deluge

The **Hawaiian** people, who are part of the broader **Polynesian** cultural family, also have rich oral traditions that include several flood myths. One of the central flood myths in Hawaiian culture is the story of **Nu'u**, a figure who is said to have survived a great flood that wiped out all life on the islands. This myth, like others in Polynesian cultures, involves themes of survival, divine intervention, and renewal after a cosmic disaster.

- **The Great Flood of Hawai'i**: According to the Hawaiian tradition, the gods, displeased with the actions of humanity, decide to flood the world and wipe out all living creatures. The flood is said to have been sent by the god **Kane**, who, along with his brothers, decided to destroy humanity due to the sins and transgressions of people on Earth.

- **Nu'u's Survival**: In the Hawaiian version of the flood myth, **Nu'u** is a righteous man chosen by the gods to survive the deluge. He is instructed by **Kane** to build a large **ark** (often referred to as a **"pa'a"** or "canoe" in Hawaiian), in which he and his family can take refuge. Nu'u's ark is said to have been equipped with **seeds**, animals, and **family members**, ensuring the survival of life after the floodwaters recede. The flood lasts for several days, and when the waters finally subside, Nu'u's ark comes to rest on the highest peak of the island, **Mauna Kea**, where he and his family begin the process of repopulating the Earth.

- **Divine Intervention and Renewal**: The flood in the Hawaiian myth, much like in the Māori story, is seen as a **divine intervention** intended to punish humanity's sins and **purify** the Earth. However, the survival of **Nu'u** and his family symbolizes hope for the renewal of life after the cataclysm. The flood story represents the continuous cycle of destruction and creation that is central to Hawaiian cosmology, where the Earth is periodically reborn through the actions of the gods.

Themes and Symbolism in Hawaiian Flood Myth

- **Divine Wrath and Human Survival**: Like other Polynesian flood myths, the Hawaiian tale of **Nu'u** emphasizes the role of the gods in shaping the fate of humanity. The flood is both a punishment for human transgressions and an opportunity for **spiritual renewal**. The ark, as a symbol of survival and preservation, reflects the idea that life, in all its forms, is protected by the divine for a greater purpose.

- **Cleansing and Rebirth**: The flood's primary function in Hawaiian mythology is the **cleansing** of the Earth. As with the Māori myth, the flood clears the world of corruption and **sin**, making way for the regeneration of life. After the floodwaters recede, life begins anew, with **Nu'u** and his family tasked with the responsibility of repopulating the Earth and restoring order.

- **Connection to Actual Natural Disasters**: The Hawaiian islands, like other parts of the Pacific, are prone to natural disasters such as **tsunamis, earthquakes**, and **volcanic eruptions**. These events may have shaped the flood myth as a way to explain the cyclical nature of these destructive forces. The flood story serves as a symbolic expression of the impact of these natural events on the people of the islands.

3. Similarities with Other Flood Myths

The flood myths of the **Māori** and **Hawaiian** peoples share many similarities with other ancient flood myths found across the globe. These common themes include:

- **Divine Punishment**: Flood myths often feature a deity or deities sending a flood to punish humanity for its actions, whether through corruption, sin, or disobedience. This theme is common in many cultures, from the **Mesopotamian** story of **Gilgamesh** to the **Biblical** flood of **Noah's Ark**.

- **Survival and Restoration**: Another recurring theme is the survival of a single individual or family chosen by the gods to repopulate and restore the Earth. This idea of **divine selection** mirrors the survival of figures like **Noah** in the Bible, **Utnapishtim** in the **Epic of Gilgamesh**, and **Manu** in Hindu tradition.

- **Cosmic Rebirth**: Following the flood, many myths portray the renewal of life and the restoration of order. This **rebirth** after destruction is central to the understanding of the cycles of creation and destruction that characterize many flood myths.

The flood myths of the **Māori** and **Hawaiian** peoples, like those from other parts of the world, are deeply rooted in the **cultural memory** of ancient cataclysmic events. These myths reflect a shared understanding of the **interconnectedness** between humanity, the gods, and the natural world. They also offer a powerful reminder of the importance of harmony with nature and the need to **respect the forces** that shape the environment. As with other flood myths, these stories suggest that the Pacific Islanders may have been interpreting the catastrophic effects of **rising sea levels**, **tsunamis**, or **global climate shifts**, events that could have been linked to the end of the **Ice Age** or other environmental upheavals. Through these myths, the people of the Pacific Islands preserved their collective memory of such transformative events, passing down valuable lessons of survival, moral renewal, and cosmic balance for generations.

Chapter 19: Flood Stories from Africa: From the Dogon to the Zulu

Africa is a vast continent, home to a diverse array of cultures, languages, and traditions. Among the many fascinating aspects of African cultures are the rich oral traditions, which include stories that explain the natural world and humanity's relationship to it. Flood myths, like those found in other parts of the world, are a prominent feature in African mythology, particularly in cultures from West and Southern Africa. These myths, although unique in their specific details, share universal themes such as **divine punishment**, **cosmic destruction**, and **the renewal of life** after a cataclysmic flood. By exploring African flood stories, we can gain insight into how these cultures viewed natural disasters, human nature, and the cyclical nature of life.

This chapter will explore two prominent African flood myths from the **Dogon people** of Mali (West Africa) and the **Zulu people** of Southern Africa, examining how these stories reflect ancient cultural memories of global catastrophes such as **rising waters**, **catastrophic storms**, or the possible impact events related to the Younger Dryas period.

---

1. The Dogon Flood Myth: The Descent of the Nommo

The **Dogon people** of Mali are renowned for their complex cosmology and spiritual beliefs, many of which have been passed down through generations in oral tradition. Their flood myth is tied to their cosmological understanding of the world and the **Nommo**, water deities who are central to their creation narrative. The Dogon flood myth is not as widely known as others, but it holds great significance in understanding their worldview.

The Nommo and the Great Deluge

In Dogon mythology, the **Nommo** are ancestral spirits, often described as half-human, half-fish beings, who are said to have arrived from the **Sirius star system**. The **Nommo** are believed to have descended to Earth from the skies, bringing with them knowledge of agriculture, water, and life. The flood myth is intricately linked to the **Nommo** and their role in the creation of the world. According to the Dogon, after the Nommo descended from the heavens, they brought with them **life-giving water** and taught humanity the importance of **rituals, agriculture,** and **the cycles of nature**.

- **The Cataclysm and the Flood**: The Dogon flood myth centers around a catastrophic event when the Nommo left the Earth in response to human corruption or failure to respect cosmic order. This departure is said to have been followed by a devastating flood, which was seen as a **divine punishment** for humanity's moral decline. The flood submerged the Earth, cleansing it and resetting the world. The water returned to the land as a means of restoring balance and purifying the world.

- **Survival and Rebirth**: The flood was not intended to annihilate all life, but rather to serve as a purification, with only a few survivors left to repopulate the world. The survivors of the flood were thought to have been protected by the **Nommo** or hidden in the highest regions of the earth. This act of divine intervention symbolizes the idea of **rebirth**, as the floodwaters receded, and life began anew, just as it had before the **Nommo**'s departure.

Symbolism and Meaning of the Dogon Flood Myth

- **Water as a Purifier**: The flood in Dogon mythology is seen as a means of **purification**, much like other global flood myths. Water is not merely destructive; it is a force of **cosmic order** that renews the world and makes way for the continuation of life. The **Nommo** represent the vital force of water, which sustains all living things but can also overwhelm and cleanse the Earth if humanity loses its way.

- **Cosmic Balance and Punishment**: The flood serves as a reminder of the importance of balance in the universe. Just as the Nommo taught humanity to respect the laws of nature, the flood represents the consequences of failing to live in harmony with these laws. The destruction caused by the flood is a reflection of the divine anger but also an opportunity for humanity to learn from its mistakes.

- **The Nommo's Departure**: The departure of the Nommo symbolizes a severance from divine knowledge and guidance. The flood marks a moment in the Dogon people's history when they lost their connection to the gods, but the myth also reflects a yearning for a return to divine wisdom.

2. The Zulu Flood Myth: Unkulunkulu and the Deluge

The **Zulu people**, one of the largest ethnic groups in Southern Africa, have a rich oral tradition and an intricate cosmology. Their creation myths, which involve the supreme god **Unkulunkulu**, the ancestors, and various spirits, contain several stories that reflect the cycles of nature, including **flood myths**.

The Creation of the World and the First Flood

The Zulu creation story centers on **Unkulunkulu**, who is believed to be the creator of humanity and the world. According to Zulu myth, Unkulunkulu first created the **earth**, the **sky**, and **all living creatures**, including humans. However, humans, in their early state, lived in a chaotic and disordered world. As a result of their disobedience and corruption, the gods decided to punish them with a **great flood**.

- **Unkulunkulu's Anger**: The flood is said to have been sent by **Unkulunkulu** as a means of punishing humanity for its transgressions. The human race had failed to honor the gods and had become morally corrupt, leading Unkulunkulu to decide that only a great flood could restore order and purity to the world. The flood is described as a massive **downpour of rain**, inundating the Earth and wiping out most of humanity.

- **The Survivors**: However, not all of humanity perished in the flood. A **single family** or small group of people survived, often through divine intervention or because they were favored by Unkulunkulu. After the floodwaters subsided, these survivors were tasked with repopulating the Earth, thus restarting the cycle of human life. In some versions of the myth, a single man and his family are saved in a **boat-like vessel** or a **shelter**, similar to Noah's Ark in other traditions.

Themes and Symbolism in the Zulu Flood Myth

- **Divine Punishment and Moral Lessons**: Like many other African and global flood myths, the Zulu story emphasizes the role of **divine punishment** for human wrongdoing. The flood represents a cleansing of the Earth, where the gods use water as a tool to **restore cosmic order**. The **moral lessons** inherent in the story stress the importance of respecting the divine laws and living harmoniously with nature.

- **Cosmic Rebirth and Renewal**: The Zulu myth, like others, contains themes of **renewal** after catastrophe. The flood is not the end of the world but a necessary event that paves the way for a new beginning. The survivors are seen as the **ancestors** of future generations, and their survival symbolizes the resilience and **rebirth** of life after disaster.

- **Connection to Natural Disasters**: The Zulu flood myth, as with many others, may be a symbolic representation of real-world events such as **floods** or **seasonal rains** that the people would have witnessed. Southern Africa is subject to **periods of intense rainfall** and **droughts**, both of which can lead to significant flooding and destruction. These natural phenomena may have influenced the development of the flood myth in Zulu culture.

---

3. Similarities with Other Global Flood Myths

Both the **Dogon** and **Zulu** flood myths share many elements with other ancient flood myths found around the world:

- **Divine Retribution**: In both cultures, the flood is sent by a supreme god as punishment for human corruption or failure to live according to divine laws. This is a common theme in many flood myths, including those of the **Bible, Sumeria**, and **Hinduism**.

- **Survival and Rebirth**: Like other flood myths, both the Dogon and Zulu stories emphasize the survival of a small group of people, often chosen by the gods. These survivors are tasked with repopulating the Earth, symbolizing **renewal** and **rebirth**.

- **Water as a Cleansing Force**: In both the Dogon and Zulu traditions, water is seen not just as a destructive force, but as a **purifier** that cleanses the Earth and prepares it for a new cycle of life. This reflects the understanding that natural forces, such as floods, are both destructive and regenerative.

The flood myths of the **Dogon** and **Zulu** peoples, like those from other cultures, serve as powerful symbols of **cosmic order**, **moral lessons**, and **natural cycles**. These myths reflect the deep connection that African cultures have to the **natural world** and their understanding of the forces of nature as both destructive and regenerative. The stories also provide valuable insight into the **historical memory** of possible natural disasters, such as **rising floodwaters** or **climate shifts**, that may have had a profound impact on ancient societies. Ultimately, these flood myths reinforce the idea of humanity's responsibility to live in harmony with the forces of nature and the divine, a theme that resonates across cultures and generations.

Part IV: The Younger Dryas and the Evidence of Water

Chapter 23: Meltwater and Rising Seas: Geological Evidence of Cataclysmic Flooding

The idea of a great flood is a recurring theme in cultures around the world. While many of these stories are embedded in myth and legend, there is also compelling **geological evidence** suggesting that large-scale flooding events may have actually occurred in Earth's past. These events, tied to the end of the **Last Ice Age** and the onset of the **Holocene Epoch**, may have contributed to the development of flood myths across different cultures. Specifically, the **meltwater pulses** and **rapid sea-level rise** that occurred at the end of the **Pleistocene** provide geological evidence for catastrophic flooding events. This chapter will explore the **scientific evidence** for these phenomena, as well as how they might correlate with global flood myths, providing a tangible link between the natural world and the cultural narratives that have emerged from it.

---

1. The Last Ice Age: Glacial Maximum and the End of the Pleistocene

To understand the significance of **meltwater pulses** and **rising seas**, it's essential to first look at the **Last Ice Age** (approximately 115,000 to 11,700 years ago). During this period, large portions of the Earth were covered by thick ice sheets, especially in regions like **North America**, **Europe**, and **Asia**. These ice sheets held vast amounts of water—water that was prevented from entering the oceans and raising sea levels.

As the Earth began to warm at the end of the Ice Age, the glaciers began to **melt**, and vast amounts of water were released into the oceans. This process had profound effects on both global sea levels and regional climates. It is this process that is believed to have caused dramatic **rising seas** and **cataclysmic flooding**.

The Transition to the Holocene and Sea-Level Rise

At the end of the Ice Age, around **11,700 years ago**, the Earth entered the **Holocene Epoch**, a period of warming that saw the glaciers retreat. As the ice sheets melted, the global sea levels began to rise at an accelerated rate. During this transition, the planet experienced a series of **rapid** meltwater pulses—moments when the rate of sea-level rise sharply increased, flooding coastal areas and reshaping the environment.

2. Meltwater Pulses: Sudden and Catastrophic Flooding

Meltwater pulses refer to sudden and massive releases of freshwater from the melting ice sheets, which caused rapid sea-level rise. The most significant meltwater pulses occurred around **14,500 years ago** and **8,000 years ago**, and these events had profound geological effects. Here are the main meltwater pulses that are believed to have corresponded with global flooding events:

Meltwater Pulse 1A (~14,500 years ago)

One of the most significant and well-documented meltwater pulses, **Meltwater Pulse 1A**, occurred at the end of the **Younger Dryas** period, a time of sudden cooling that preceded the warming of the Holocene. During this pulse, **sea levels rose by about 16 to 20 meters (52 to 66 feet)** in less than 500 years. This represents a **cataclysmic rise** that could have dramatically flooded coastal areas, displacing human populations and altering landscapes across large regions.

- **Impact on Landscapes**: The rapid rise in sea levels would have submerged vast coastal plains, drowned river valleys, and altered the course of rivers. Major flood plains like the **Beringia Land Bridge**, the **Doggerland** region (now beneath the North Sea), and parts of **North America** would have been swamped by the encroaching seas. In some areas, these changes in sea level would have reshaped coastlines almost overnight.

- **Connection with Flood Myths**: The **suddenness** and **magnitude** of this rise in sea level could very well explain the origins of flood myths, particularly those that describe **divine retribution** or **cosmic destruction**. These mythological stories often involve a great flood that occurs **unexpectedly** and overwhelms humanity, aligning with the reality of a rapid, catastrophic event in Earth's geological history.

Meltwater Pulse 1B (~8,000 years ago)

Another significant meltwater event occurred around **8,000 years ago**, though this pulse was less extreme than **Meltwater Pulse 1A**. However, it still resulted in a notable rise in sea levels, estimated to be around **5 to 10** meters. This second pulse likely occurred as the **Laurentide Ice Sheet** in North America continued to melt, as well as other ice sheets in the Northern Hemisphere.

- **Impact on Human Populations**: By this time, human populations were already establishing more permanent settlements along coastlines, and the rising sea levels would have likely displaced these communities, forcing them to move or adapt to new environments. The memory of such displacements may have been preserved in flood myths passed down through generations.

---

3. Evidence of Cataclysmic Flooding: Geological and Archaeological Data

The geological evidence for these rapid meltwater pulses and rising seas is derived from a variety of scientific sources, including **sediment cores, ice cores, marine isotopes, and paleoclimatic data**. These data sources provide direct evidence of the environmental changes that took place at the end of the Ice Age.

Sediment Cores and Sea-Level Indicators

Researchers have collected **sediment cores** from the ocean floor and from coastal regions that were once landmasses but were subsequently flooded due to rising sea levels. These cores provide valuable information about past sea levels, such as:

- **Stratigraphy**: Layers of sediment in these cores can show distinct transitions from dry land to submerged landscapes. By analyzing these layers, scientists can estimate the timing and rate of sea-level rise.

- **Fossil Evidence**: Fossils of **marine organisms** found in these sediment layers provide clues about the environments that existed before the flooding. For example, the sudden appearance of marine species in formerly terrestrial sediment layers can indicate a rapid and significant rise in sea levels.

- **Isotopic Analysis**: Researchers also use **isotopic signatures** found in ocean cores to understand past sea levels. Changes in the **oxygen**

isotopes of marine shells, corals, and foraminifera can help scientists track shifts in sea levels and temperature.

Archaeological Evidence

Archaeological findings in coastal areas also provide evidence of how human populations may have been impacted by these events. For example:

- **Submerged Settlements**: Some archaeological sites, such as those found in the **North Sea** (Doggerland), have been submerged by rising sea levels. These sites reveal evidence of ancient human habitation that was lost due to flooding. Similar submerged sites have been discovered off the coasts of **India**, **Japan**, and the **Caribbean**.

- **Artifacts and Tools**: Archaeological discoveries of tools and artifacts in areas that were once coastal suggest that humans lived in these areas before being displaced by rising seas. The sudden disappearance of certain cultures or populations could correlate with the rapid flooding events of the Younger Dryas and the subsequent meltwater pulses.

---

4. Connecting Geological Events to Flood Myths

The rapid sea-level rise associated with meltwater pulses, particularly the **Younger Dryas**, aligns closely with the stories of sudden, catastrophic flooding found in many global mythologies. The geographical areas that were flooded—such as the **Bering Land Bridge, Doggerland**, and the **Sundaland** region—correspond to regions where flood myths are particularly strong, suggesting a direct link between actual catastrophic events and the stories that emerged in these cultures.

Global Flood Mythology and Meltwater Pulses

Many flood myths describe a **cataclysmic deluge** that covers the Earth or submerges entire civilizations. In some cases, these myths describe survivors who flee to higher ground or are saved in boats. These stories could be rooted in the memories of populations who were affected by rapid sea-level rise and the flooding of previously inhabited coastal areas.

- **Sumerian and Biblical Floods**: The **Sumerian** and **Biblical** flood myths, which describe a divine flood wiping out all of humanity except for a select few survivors, may be echoes of this rapid flooding caused by meltwater pulses. The specific details of these myths—such as the building of an ark or the survival of a small group of people—are consistent with a large-scale inundation event.
- **Indigenous Flood Stories**: Indigenous cultures around the world, from **Native American tribes** to **Polynesian societies**, have flood stories that may preserve collective memories of such events. For example, the **Hopi** people of North America have oral traditions that speak of a great flood, which many scholars have linked to environmental changes at the end of the Ice Age.

The connection between **meltwater pulses** and **rising sea levels** at the end of the Ice Age and the **flood myths** of various cultures is an example of how **geological evidence** can shed light on the origins of ancient stories. These global myths are likely rooted in real events—catastrophic floods caused by **rapid sea-level rise**, which overwhelmed early human settlements. As these events became ingrained in cultural memory, they were transformed into powerful myths that were passed down through generations.

By examining the **geological evidence** of meltwater pulses, **archaeological findings**, and **climatic data**, we gain a deeper understanding of how ancient peoples might have experienced and remembered such cataclysmic events. The flood myths of the world, when viewed in the context of these geological events, represent not only the power of **nature** but also humanity's ability to adapt, survive, and learn from catastrophic disasters.

Chapter 24: Glacial Lakes and the Mega-Floods

One of the most dramatic consequences of the end of the Ice Age was the formation of **glacial lakes**—massive bodies of water that were trapped behind the receding ice sheets. These lakes held enormous quantities of water, and their eventual rupture led to **mega-floods,** which reshaped landscapes and left a lasting imprint on both the environment and human history. This chapter will explore the formation of **glacial lakes**, the catastrophic **outbursts** that resulted from their collapse, and the implications these events have for our understanding of **flood myths** and **climatic cataclysms** at the close of the last Ice Age.

---

1. The Formation of Glacial Lakes

As the vast **ice sheets** that covered much of the Earth during the **Pleistocene Epoch** began to melt at the end of the Ice Age, large amounts of water were temporarily trapped by the remnants of glaciers. The **glacial lakes** formed in regions where the ice had retreated, leaving behind natural dams of ice, sediment, and rock. These lakes could span thousands of square miles and contain more water than many of today's largest rivers.

Some of the largest and most famous of these **glacial lakes** include:

- **Lake Missoula**: Located in present-day **Montana, Lake Missoula** was formed by the **Purcell Trench** glacier. This lake could have contained up to 2,000 cubic miles of water, held in place by a massive **ice dam**. When the dam eventually failed, it triggered one of the most dramatic flood events in Earth's history—the **Missoula Floods**.

- **Lake Agassiz**: This was one of the largest glacial lakes in **North America**, covering much of present-day **Canada** and parts of the northern United States. It was formed by the melting of the **Laurentide Ice Sheet**. The sudden outbursts from Lake Agassiz, particularly its final collapse, are believed to have caused **massive flooding** in the surrounding regions.

- **Glacial Lake Iroquois**: This lake was located in present-day **Ontario** and parts of **New York State**. It was formed by the **Wisconsin Glaciation** and had significant implications for regional landscapes when it burst.

---

2. The Catastrophic Outbursts: Mega-Floods

The **catastrophic outbursts** of these glacial lakes, also known as **mega-floods**, represent some of the largest and most destructive flood events in Earth's history. The collapse of the ice dams that held the waters in these lakes would often result in **massive, rapid discharges** of water, enough to reshape valleys, carve out canyons, and deposit enormous amounts of sediment over vast regions. These floods were not slow, gradual events—they were **instantaneous** and **unpredictable**, releasing energy equivalent to that of **hundreds of times the flow of all the world's rivers combined**.

The **Missoula Floods** and other mega-floods are particularly famous for their **devastating effects** on the landscape. Let's examine how these floods occurred:

The Missoula Floods (14,000–15,000 years ago)

One of the most well-known and studied examples of a **mega-flood** is the **Missoula Floods**. These catastrophic events were caused by the rupture of the **ice dam** that held back the waters of **Lake Missoula**. The dam was located in the **Clark Fork River Valley** in present-day **Montana**.

- **Flood Event**: When the ice dam failed, the **glacial lake**—which had accumulated immense amounts of water—was unleashed in a matter of hours, sending a torrent of water across the **Columbia Plateau** in **Washington State**. The flooding created the **Channeled Scablands**, a unique and rugged landscape characterized by deep canyons, scoured bedrock, and **giant ripples** formed by the force of the water.

- **Flowing at Unprecedented Speeds**: The **Missoula Floods** sent water rushing at speeds of up to **60 miles per hour** (97 km/h), carrying **sediment** and debris with it. The waterflow was so powerful that it eroded solid rock and left behind **giant boulders**, some weighing as much as several tons, that were carried for hundreds of miles.

- **Environmental Consequences**: The floods reshaped the environment, creating new waterways, depressions, and floodplains, while completely altering the ecology of the region. The floodwaters would have rapidly inundated large areas, drowning wildlife, plants, and human settlements, if they had been present in the region at the time. The devastation caused by these floods is consistent with the themes of **cataclysmic floods** found in mythological stories from many cultures.

Other Notable Mega-Floods

- **Lake Agassiz and the Laurentide Ice Sheet**: In the **northern United States and Canada**, the collapse of **Lake Agassiz** caused a massive outburst flood that flowed down the **Mississippi River Valley**. This event is thought to have triggered **dramatic changes** in the climate and environment, including the sudden shift from the cold **Younger Dryas** to the warmer **Holocene**.

- **The Great Floods of the British Isles**: As the glaciers retreated across northern **Europe**, large bodies of water formed behind the ice sheets. The collapse of these glacial lakes flooded **vast regions** of what is now **Britain**, **Ireland**, and parts of **Scandinavia**. These floods would have reshaped the coastline and led to the submerging of land bridges that once connected the islands to the mainland.

---

3. Geological Evidence of Mega-Floods

There is significant **geological evidence** of the catastrophic events caused by these glacial lake outbursts. Researchers have studied the **landforms** and **sediment deposits** left behind by these mega-floods, which provide key insights into their scale and impact.

Scablands and Erosional Features

The **Channeled Scablands** in Washington State, formed by the **Missoula Floods**, provide some of the clearest evidence of ancient mega-floods. The **flood channels** carved into the landscape are visible today as **deep, wide valleys**, and the **giant ripples**—large, wave-like formations on the bedrock—are direct evidence of the immense energy released during the floods.

Boulder Bars and Erratics

Floodwaters from these events deposited **giant boulders** and **erratics** (large rocks carried from distant locations by floodwaters). In many regions that experienced mega-floods, scattered boulders can still be found far from their source areas. These stones, sometimes weighing several tons, were carried by the floodwaters and deposited in places that show evidence of the **force** of the floods.

Sediment Layers and Deposits

In areas affected by glacial lake outbursts, researchers have found **distinct layers of sediment** that reflect rapid deposition of materials, such as **sand**, **silt**, and **gravel**. These deposits are often laid down in **widespread sheets**, covering large areas in a short period of time, which is consistent with the rapid flooding that occurred.

Marine Fossils in Freshwater Locations

In some cases, **marine fossils** have been found in freshwater sediments that were deposited during the flood events, providing evidence of how **coastal regions** were submerged by the rising floodwaters, which would have reached **sea level** in many regions.

---

4. Flood Myths and Mega-Floods

The **mega-floods** caused by glacial lake outbursts were cataclysmic events, and it is not surprising that many ancient cultures preserved memories of such events in their **flood myths**. The sudden and overwhelming nature of these floods—especially the **Missoula Floods**—might have inspired stories of great deluges that wiped out entire civilizations.

- **The Missoula Floods and Native American Legends**: Indigenous tribes living in the **Pacific Northwest**, particularly the **Nez Perce** and **Colville** tribes, have oral traditions that describe massive floods that reshaped the landscape. These stories may be rooted in the memory of the **Missoula Floods**, which occurred relatively recently in human history (approximately 14,000 years ago).

- **Flood Myths from Other Cultures**: The stories of **Noah's Ark** in the Bible, the **Epic of Gilgamesh**, and other ancient flood tales may have been inspired by actual **cataclysmic flooding** events that occurred at the end of the Ice Age. These stories often involve divine intervention and the preservation of a select few survivors, reflecting the chaos and destruction wrought by massive floods.

The collapse of **glacial lakes** and the resulting **mega-floods** marked a pivotal moment in Earth's geological history, reshaping the environment in ways that would have had profound effects on ancient human societies. The sudden, catastrophic nature of these floods left a lasting imprint on the land, creating features that can still be seen today, such as **scablands**, **boulder bars**, and **sediment deposits**.

These events were not merely geological phenomena—they also became **cultural touchstones**. The memories of these overwhelming floods were passed down through generations, preserved in **myths** and **legends** that echo the catastrophic nature of the floods themselves. Understanding the **scientific evidence** behind these floods allows us to see how deeply intertwined **human experience** and **natural events** can be, and how **geological catastrophes** may have shaped the myths that continue to influence our understanding of the world.

Chapter 26: The Black Sea Flood: A Real-World Connection

The **Black Sea flood** is one of the most fascinating and controversial theories that attempt to link a **real-world catastrophe** with **ancient flood myths**, including the **biblical story of Noah's Ark**. This catastrophic event, which occurred around 7,500 years ago, is believed to have had a profound impact on the region surrounding the Black Sea, potentially providing a historical basis for many of the world's flood legends. This chapter delves into the evidence supporting the **Black Sea flood hypothesis**, its geological and archaeological significance, and how it might have influenced flood myths in ancient cultures.

1. The Geological Evidence for the Black Sea Flood

The idea that the **Black Sea** experienced a sudden, catastrophic flooding event is based on a range of geological and archaeological evidence. This flood is theorized to have occurred during the transition from the **Pleistocene** to the **Holocene**—around **7,500 years ago**—a period when sea levels were rising rapidly as the Ice Age ended and glaciers melted.

The Black Sea Before the Flood

At the time, the Black Sea was originally a **small, isolated freshwater lake** surrounded by land, with the **Bosporus Strait** (now the connection between the Black Sea and the **Mediterranean**) closed off by land. The Black Sea was primarily freshwater, fed by rivers such as the **Danube**, **Dniester**, and **Dnieper**. Over time, as the glaciers retreated at the end of the last Ice Age, sea levels around the world began to rise.

The Breaching of the Bosporus

The most widely accepted theory suggests that the rising **Mediterranean Sea** eventually overwhelmed the natural dam of land that separated the Black Sea from the sea to the south, **resulting in a catastrophic breach**. The **Bosporus Strait**, which connects the Black Sea to the Mediterranean, is believed to have been an **ancient land bridge** before this event. As the Mediterranean waters surged northward, they flooded the lower-lying regions around the Black Sea.

- **Flood Event**: Once the breach occurred, the **Mediterranean Sea** poured into the Black Sea at an unprecedented rate, creating a **massive flood**. The flood is believed to have occurred over the course of **months or even years**, with seawater rising as much as **100 meters (328 feet)** in a short period of time. The rapid influx of saltwater transformed the once-freshwater lake into the brackish and saltwater Black Sea we know today.

- **Magnitude of the Flood**: The sheer magnitude of this event would have caused **dramatic environmental and societal upheaval**. The floodwaters would have swept away entire villages, devastated ecosystems, and inundated land that had been home to **early human settlements**. This transformation of the Black Sea from a freshwater lake to a saltwater sea is marked by a clear **change in sediment layers** and evidence of the flooding in the region's coastline and underwater topography.

---

2. Archaeological Evidence of the Black Sea Flood

Several lines of archaeological evidence support the theory of a catastrophic flood in the Black Sea:

Underwater Settlements

In the 1990s, **marine archaeologists** began exploring the floor of the Black Sea and made remarkable discoveries of **ancient settlements** submerged by the floodwaters. At depths of around **100 meters**, near the modern-day Bosporus Strait, researchers discovered signs of ancient **human habitation**, including **stone tools**, **structures**, and **pottery**. These sites were clearly submerged after the time when the area was occupied, suggesting that the rise in sea levels must have been rapid and massive.

- **Site of an Ancient Shoreline**: The submerged sites appear to correspond to an **ancient shoreline**, indicating that the land around the Black Sea was once much lower, and the region was populated before the flood occurred. The evidence points to a **gradual drowning** of these settlements over time, as the floodwaters from the Mediterranean moved northward.

- **A Shift in Ecosystems**: Before the flooding event, the Black Sea was primarily a freshwater environment. The archaeological sites show evidence of a thriving, pre-flood **fishing economy**, where the ancient people used local freshwater fish as their primary resource. The flood that followed would have **disrupted** this economy and forced early communities to **adapt** or relocate.

Sediment Layers and Geological Evidence

Geologists have identified a **distinct sediment layer** beneath the Black Sea, marking a clear divide between **freshwater** and **saltwater** conditions. This boundary layer, often referred to as the **Black Sea Flood Layer**, is rich in **marine fossils**, indicating the transformation from a freshwater lake to a saltwater sea. This sudden environmental shift aligns with the timeline of the hypothesized flood, further supporting the theory that a massive inundation occurred.

- **Carbon Dating**: Carbon dating of organic materials found in the flood sediments has placed the event at approximately **7,500 years ago**, aligning with the cultural and archaeological timeline of ancient human settlements in the region. This further strengthens the argument that the flooding of the Black Sea was a significant and cataclysmic event that left its mark on ancient societies.

3. The Connection to Flood Myths: A Global Phenomenon

The sudden and catastrophic flooding of the Black Sea likely had a profound impact on the people living around its shores, and the memory of this event may have been passed down through **oral traditions** and ultimately woven into the fabric of **flood myths** found across cultures. One of the most famous of these myths is the biblical **story of Noah's Ark**, but the theme of a great flood can be found in numerous cultures worldwide.

Noah's Ark and the Black Sea Flood

The **biblical flood story** in the **Book of Genesis** describes a great deluge sent by God to destroy all life on Earth, with **Noah** and his family surviving by taking refuge in an ark filled with pairs of animals. The floodwaters eventually recede, and Noah's ark comes to rest on the **Mount Ararat**.

Many scholars have speculated that the **Noah's Ark** narrative may have been inspired by an actual flooding event, such as the one that occurred in the Black Sea region. Some key parallels include:

- **Sudden, Unpredictable Flood**: The Black Sea flood likely appeared to the people living around the coast as an overwhelming, **unpredictable event**, where entire landscapes and settlements were swallowed by the rising waters. This fits the **biblical narrative** of a flood that came suddenly, wiping out humanity except for Noah and his family.

- **Survival and Preservation**: The idea of **preserving life** during the flood, as seen in Noah's Ark, could have been a symbolic representation of humanity's attempt to survive such a massive natural disaster. In some versions of the Black Sea flood narrative, it is believed that early settlers took refuge on higher ground or constructed **floating shelters** to survive the deluge.

- **A Return to Normalcy**: After the floodwaters receded, life in the Black Sea region would have been forever changed. The new coastline and ecosystems would have forced survivors to adapt to the new environment, much like the post-flood world described in the Genesis story.

Other Flood Myths: Shared Cultural Memory?

The Black Sea flood also helps explain the **similarities** between flood myths across different cultures. The presence of **flood myths** in ancient cultures from the **Sumerians** to the **Maya**, the **Hindu traditions** to the **Chinese**, and **Native American legends** to **Polynesian stories** suggests a shared **cultural memory** of a catastrophic flood event. While the specifics of the mythologies differ, the core theme of a **great deluge** and the survival of a select few survivors seems to be universal.

- **The Epic of Gilgamesh**: The Sumerian account of a great flood in the **Epic of Gilgamesh**, written around 2100 BCE, is remarkably similar to the story of Noah's Ark. In the myth, the hero **Utnapishtim** is instructed by the gods to build a boat to survive a flood that will wipe out humanity. This flood story predates the biblical Noah's story and may share common roots with regional flooding events, including the Black Sea flood.

- **Other Cultures**: Similar flood myths in the **Maya** of Mesoamerica, the **Hindu** tradition of Manu's flood, and **Native American** traditions further suggest that the story of a cataclysmic flood is not isolated to any one culture but is a recurring theme that may stem from shared memories of real-world events.

The **Black Sea flood** theory provides a compelling connection between real-world geological events and ancient flood myths. The catastrophic inundation of the Black Sea around **7,500 years ago** would have had a profound effect on the **early human populations** living in the region, and the event likely left a lasting imprint on their collective memories. These memories were passed down through oral traditions and eventually became embedded in the **flood myths** that have been shared across cultures for millennia.

Understanding the **Black Sea flood** not only sheds light on the **geological history** of the region but also offers insights into the **origins of flood myths**, especially the biblical story of Noah's Ark. By connecting real-world catastrophic events with the myths of ancient peoples, we gain a deeper understanding of how humans have interpreted and recorded the profound natural disasters that have shaped our world throughout history.

Chapter 27: The Ice Dams and the End of the Ice Age

The transition from the **Ice Age** to the **Holocene** epoch, which began around **12,000 years ago**, was marked by dramatic climatic shifts, including the sudden cooling of the **Younger Dryas** and the eventual warming that heralded the end of the Ice Age. One of the most important and influential processes contributing to these changes were the **melting ice dams**, which played a crucial role in triggering massive floods and shifts in global climate. In this chapter, we explore the **formation of ice dams**, their catastrophic release, and how they may have been key drivers of climate change at the close of the Pleistocene.

---

1. The Formation of Ice Dams

At the peak of the **Ice Age,** large portions of the Northern Hemisphere were covered by massive glaciers, often referred to as the **Laurentide Ice Sheet** (in North America), the **Fennoscandian Ice Sheet** (in northern Europe), and the **Patagonian Ice Sheet** (in South America). These glaciers were huge and held enormous amounts of freshwater, which, as they began to melt, created significant shifts in the environment.

Ice Dams and Glacial Lakes

As the glaciers began to retreat due to **climate warming**, they left behind vast bodies of water trapped by ice barriers. These ice barriers acted as **natural dams**, preventing the meltwater from draining away. These lakes, often referred to as **glacial lakes**, were **temporary** but incredibly massive, holding **millions of cubic kilometers** of water. Examples of such glacial lakes include:

- **Lake Missoula** (in North America)
- **Lake Agassiz** (in North America)
- **Lake Iroquois** (in North America)
- **Lake Bonneville** (in North America)

These lakes were typically located in areas where glaciers had carved deep depressions in the land, creating large basins. The ice dams were formed when the glaciers themselves or thick ice sheets blocked the natural drainage of these lakes. The water accumulated in these lakes, often reaching dangerous levels, and the dammed water could not escape easily

The Fragility of Ice Dams

Though these ice dams were large and formidable, they were inherently unstable. The dynamics of glacial melting and the sheer weight of the water behind them created pressure that, over time, weakened the ice barrier. Small changes in temperature or movement of the glacier could lead to the **collapse** of these ice dams, releasing immense volumes of water in a short period of time.

---

2. The Cataclysmic Floods: Breaching the Ice Dams

When these ice dams eventually breached, the result was nothing short of a **cataclysmic flood**. The release of water from these lakes was often rapid and violent, leading to massive **flood events** that reshaped the landscape and had lasting environmental and climatic consequences.

The Lake Missoula Floods

One of the most famous examples of a catastrophic flood caused by the breaching of an ice dam was the series of floods from **Lake Missoula**, located in what is now **Montana**, USA. The **Lake Missoula flood**, also known as the **Glacial Lake Missoula flood**, occurred around **13,000 to 15,000 years ago** at the end of the last Ice Age.

- **Ice Dam Failure**: The ice dam holding back Lake Missoula was formed by the **Purcell Mountains**. As the glacier slowly melted, the dam would often weaken. When the dam eventually broke, the floodwaters rushed out at an astonishing rate, carving out large portions of the **Channeled Scablands** in eastern Washington and leaving behind giant **scour marks** on the landscape.

- **Flood Magnitude**: The Lake Missoula flood was one of the largest floods in Earth's history. It is estimated that the flood released **several hundred cubic miles** of water, enough to cover the entire state of Washington in 400 feet of water. The waters rushed across the land at speeds of up to **60 miles per hour** (97 kilometers per hour), carrying debris, boulders, and sediment, reshaping the terrain and leaving behind **massive sedimentary deposits**.

- **Impact on Human Populations**: These sudden floods would have had a profound effect on early human populations living in the area. It is likely that the force of the floods wiped out settlements and ecosystems, changing the landscape permanently. This catastrophic event may also have contributed to **myths and legends** of giant floods that are found in many cultures.

Lake Agassiz Flooding

Another significant event caused by ice dam failure was the catastrophic flooding associated with **Lake Agassiz**, a massive glacial lake that existed in what is now **Canada** and parts of the northern United States. At its peak, Lake Agassiz covered much of present-day **Manitoba, Ontario**, and parts of the **Dakotas**. The lake was formed by the **Laurentide Ice Sheet**, and its outburst floods had a global impact on both the environment and climate.

- **Cataclysmic Breaches**: The release of water from Lake Agassiz occurred in stages, with several large floods sending water across what is now the northern **Mississippi River** and eventually into the **Atlantic Ocean** via the **St. Lawrence Seaway**. The breach of the ice dam led to rapid, catastrophic discharges of water into the North Atlantic, possibly affecting ocean currents and contributing to the sudden cooling event known as the **Younger Dryas**.

- **Climate Impact**: The floodwaters from Lake Agassiz would have had a significant impact on global climate. The massive influx of freshwater into the North Atlantic likely disrupted the **Atlantic Meridional Overturning Circulation (AMOC)**, which plays a key role in regulating Earth's climate. A disruption of the AMOC could have led to the **rapid cooling** that characterized the **Younger Dryas** period, contributing to a dramatic climatic reversal that lasted over a millennium.

Lake Bonneville and the Great Salt Lake Flood

Lake Bonneville, located in present-day **Utah**, USA, was another massive glacial lake that breached its ice dam at the end of the Ice Age. The lake's catastrophic outburst, known as the **Bonneville Flood**, occurred around **14,500 years ago** and released water into the **Great Basin**.

- **Outburst Dynamics**: The floodwaters from Lake Bonneville poured out through what is now known as the **Red Rock Pass**, carving a path through the land and depositing **sediment layers** along the way. The flood event reshaped the surrounding region and contributed to the formation of the **Great Salt Lake**.

- **Consequences**: Though not as large in scale as the Missoula or Agassiz floods, the **Bonneville Flood** was still a significant event in the geological record, altering landscapes and ecosystems. It also represents another example of the types of catastrophic flooding events triggered by the **melting glaciers** and **ice dams**.

---

3. The Global Climatic Impact of Ice Dam Floods

The flooding caused by the breaching of ice dams had not only **local impacts** but also far-reaching **global consequences**. As these massive lakes released their water into the oceans, they influenced ocean currents, atmospheric conditions, and global climate patterns.

Disruption of Ocean Circulation

The sudden release of massive amounts of **freshwater** into the **North Atlantic** (from events like the Lake Agassiz outburst) is believed to have disrupted the **Atlantic Meridional Overturning Circulation (AMOC)**, a key component of Earth's climate system. The AMOC is responsible for the transport of warm water from the **tropics** to the **northern latitudes**, helping to regulate temperatures in the Northern Hemisphere.

- **Cooling Event**: The influx of freshwater from these floods likely **reduced the salinity** of the ocean in the North Atlantic, weakening the AMOC and leading to the rapid cooling that defined the **Younger Dryas**. This cooling event caused **temperatures to plummet** in the Northern Hemisphere, resulting in the abrupt return of **glacial conditions** for over a thousand years.

Impact on Global Ecosystems

The rapid changes in climate caused by the outburst floods would have had significant effects on **global ecosystems**. The cooling of the Northern Hemisphere likely led to the **extinction of many species** of megafauna (such as the mammoths and mastodons) and disrupted human cultures that were already experiencing the aftermath of the Ice Age. The floods themselves, along with the climatic shifts, may have forced early human populations to **adapt** to new environments, find new food sources, and relocate to new areas.

The role of **melting ice dams** in the end of the Ice Age is a crucial component of our understanding of the transition from the **Pleistocene** to the **Holocene**. The sudden release of water from massive glacial lakes not only caused local flooding but had profound effects on the global climate. These events, such as the **Lake Missoula, Lake Agassiz,** and **Lake Bonneville** floods, were likely responsible for dramatic shifts in temperature, sea levels, and ocean currents. These catastrophic events may have contributed to the **Younger Dryas**, a sudden climate reversal that had a lasting impact on both human populations and the planet's ecosystems. The memory of these events likely lives on in the flood myths that are shared across cultures, offering a glimpse into the ancient experiences of catastrophic change.

hapter 29: The Younger Dryas Impact Crater

The **Younger Dryas** period, which lasted from approximately **12,900 to 11,700 years ago**, was a time of abrupt climate change that marked a dramatic cooling of the Earth's climate at the end of the **Pleistocene**. This cooling event was an anomaly in a broader trend of global warming that was slowly bringing the Earth out of the Ice Age. One of the leading theories for the cause of this sudden climate shift is the **Younger Dryas Impact Hypothesis**, which proposes that a **cosmic event**, such as the impact of a **comet** or **asteroid**, caused widespread environmental catastrophes, including massive wildfires, tsunamis, and cooling.

One of the most intriguing aspects of this hypothesis is the potential discovery of an **impact crater** from this event. The **Hiawatha Glacier crater** in Greenland has gained attention in recent years as a potential **impact site**, and its implications could provide valuable evidence for understanding the cataclysmic events that marked the end of the Ice Age.

This chapter explores the Hiawatha Glacier crater and the broader implications of an impact-related event during the Younger Dryas.

1. The Younger Dryas Impact Hypothesis: An Overview

Before diving into the **Hiawatha Glacier crater**, it is important to understand the basic tenets of the **Younger Dryas Impact Hypothesis**. This hypothesis suggests that a cosmic event, such as the explosion of a **comet** or the impact of an **asteroid**, occurred around **12,900 years ago**, at the onset of the Younger Dryas. This event would have released massive amounts of energy, causing a series of environmental disasters that abruptly cooled the planet.

Proponents of the hypothesis suggest that this impact:

- **Triggered massive fires**, which would have further contributed to atmospheric cooling by releasing soot into the atmosphere.
- **Created a significant disruption to the climate**, potentially sending vast amounts of water into the ocean, disrupting global ocean currents.
- **Shattered or melted ice sheets**, contributing to the release of meltwater, which could have led to the **Younger Dryas cooling period**.

The **impact hypothesis** is supported by a number of pieces of indirect evidence, including:

- **Iridium and nanodiamonds** found in sediments from the Younger Dryas period.
- **Charcoal layers**, suggesting widespread fires.
- **Meltwater pulses** that correspond with the timing of the Younger Dryas cooling event.

However, the **impact crater** itself had not been definitively identified—until the potential discovery of the Hiawatha Glacier crater in Greenland.

2. The Hiawatha Glacier Crater: Discovery and Characteristics

In **2018**, an international team of scientists discovered a **subsurface crater** beneath the **Hiawatha Glacier** in Greenland, which could potentially be linked to the Younger Dryas impact event. The crater, which was identified through a combination of **radar mapping** and **satellite imagery**, is **about 31 kilometers (19 miles)** in diameter and **more than 1 kilometer** deep.

The Discovery Process:

- **Radar Technology**: The discovery was made using **IceBridge**, a program that uses radar to map the surface and subsurface of polar regions. The radar data revealed a large, **circular depression** beneath the glacier, which suggested the presence of an impact crater.

- **Further Analysis**: Scientists initially believed the crater might be from a much older event, but subsequent research suggested it could have formed relatively recently—around **12,900 years ago**, coinciding with the Younger Dryas event.

- **Dating the Crater**: To confirm the age of the impact and its connection to the Younger Dryas, researchers would need to study **core samples** from the ice and surrounding sediments. Though this research is ongoing, the timing and size of the crater make it a compelling candidate for the source of the impact event proposed by the Younger Dryas Impact Hypothesis.

Size and Structure:

- The **Hiawatha Glacier crater** is one of the largest impact structures discovered in the Arctic and is large enough to have had a **global impact** if it was indeed caused by a cosmic event like a comet or asteroid. The sheer size of the crater suggests that the impact would have released a massive amount of energy, potentially equivalent to the explosion of a **small asteroid**.

- The structure of the crater, buried under **kilometers of ice**, makes it an intriguing candidate for a potential **cosmic impact**, as it could have released massive amounts of energy into the atmosphere, contributing to the climate disruptions associated with the Younger Dryas.

3. The Potential Impact of the Hiawatha Glacier Event

If the Hiawatha Glacier crater is linked to the Younger Dryas, the implications are far-reaching. The potential impact site offers a way to understand how an extraterrestrial event could have triggered a massive cooling period, affecting global climates and ecosystems. Here are some of the ways the event could have impacted Earth:

A Major Impact Event:

- **Comet or Asteroid Impact**: The hypothesis suggests that the impact was caused by either a **comet** or a **small asteroid**, and the crater's size suggests that the object involved was relatively large. A high-speed cosmic impact could have caused a chain reaction, creating significant environmental and atmospheric consequences. The impact itself would have likely caused **massive wildfires**, the release of **particulate matter** into the atmosphere, and a sudden disruption of global weather patterns.

- **Tsunamis and Coastal Destruction**: If the impact occurred in the ocean, it could have triggered **massive tsunamis**, affecting coastlines across the North Atlantic. These tsunamis could have devastated early human populations and ecosystems living along the coasts, contributing to the **collapse of prehistoric societies**.

Global Cooling and Climate Disruption:

- **Atmospheric and Oceanic Effects**: The impact could have injected a vast amount of debris into the atmosphere, blocking sunlight and contributing to the **cooling of the Earth**. This could explain the dramatic **temperature drop** seen during the Younger Dryas period. A **darkening of the skies** from soot and particulates would have led to a reduction in global temperatures, similar to the effects seen after large volcanic eruptions, but on a much more massive scale.

- **Meltwater and Ice Sheet Disruption**: The impact could have also caused a rapid **melting of the ice sheets**, releasing vast amounts of freshwater into the oceans. This influx of **freshwater** could have disrupted ocean currents, particularly the **Atlantic Meridional Overturning Circulation (AMOC)**, which regulates climate and temperature patterns across the Northern Hemisphere. Disrupting the AMOC could have triggered the **Younger Dryas cooling** event.

Catastrophic Effects on Ecosystems:

- **Massive Fires and Extinctions**: The debris, combined with the intense heat of the impact, could have caused widespread **wildfires** across vast areas of North America and Eurasia. These fires could have burned vast forests and altered ecosystems, leading to the extinction of megafauna like mammoths, mastodons, and saber-toothed cats. The resulting environmental collapse could have also forced early human populations to adapt to new conditions, migrate, or perish.

- **Global Ecosystem Shifts**: In addition to fires and cooling, the Younger Dryas period saw disruptions in **plant and animal life**, as ecosystems struggled to cope with rapidly changing temperatures. The cooling event would have led to a temporary reversal of the warming trend that had been occurring during the late Pleistocene, causing ecological shifts and contributing to mass extinctions.

4. Controversy and Ongoing Debate

While the **Hiawatha Glacier crater** is an exciting potential site for understanding the Younger Dryas impact event, there is still **significant debate** within the scientific community about whether this crater is indeed the source of the impact. Some challenges to the hypothesis include:

- **Lack of Direct Evidence**: While the crater is large and potentially of the right age, no direct evidence has yet been found linking it to an extraterrestrial object, such as a comet or asteroid. Researchers need more definitive **geological evidence**, such as **shock-metamorphosed minerals** or the presence of certain **chemicals** (e.g., iridium or nanodiamonds), to confirm that this is an impact site.

- **Alternative Explanations**: Some scientists suggest that the cooling associated with the Younger Dryas could be explained by factors other than a cosmic impact, such as **volcanic activity, solar variations**, or **changes in Earth's orbit**.

- **Further Research Required**: To resolve the debate, more research is needed, including drilling to obtain **sediment cores** and conducting **further geophysical surveys** of the Hiawatha Glacier region. This research will help to determine whether this crater is a product of the Younger Dryas impact event or whether it is the result of a different, older geological process.

Part V: The Aftermath: Surviving the Apocalypse

Chapter 30: The Survivors: How Human Civilizations Rebuilt After the Floods

The **Younger Dryas** event was a time of abrupt climatic upheaval that dramatically affected Earth's ecosystems, human populations, and the course of prehistory. During this period, much of the northern hemisphere experienced a sudden and severe cooling event, marked by catastrophic flooding, the extinction of megafauna, and environmental disruptions. In the aftermath of such global turmoil, the human populations that survived were faced with a vastly altered world.

This chapter explores how humanity, in the wake of such an extraordinary catastrophe, managed to adapt, rebuild, and eventually forge the civilizations that would lay the foundation for modern societies. By examining archaeological evidence, cultural developments, and the adaptive strategies of early humans, we can gain insight into how human resilience and innovation led to the rise of **agriculture**, the development of **complex societies**, and the birth of **civilizations** after the cataclysmic floods.

---

1. The Cataclysmic Aftermath: Global Environmental Changes

The Younger Dryas event is believed to have occurred around **12,900 years ago**, lasting for approximately **1,200 years**. The global cooling that accompanied this event would have drastically altered ecosystems, potentially reversing the warming trend that had been occurring during the end of the **Pleistocene Epoch**. At the same time, massive floods resulting from **meltwater pulses** from melting ice sheets would have inundated coastal areas and river valleys, displacing human populations.

Key Effects on Earth's Climate and Ecosystems:

- **Abrupt Cooling**: Average temperatures in the Northern Hemisphere dropped sharply, especially in the regions of North America and Europe. This sudden shift would have caused a collapse in plant and animal populations, disrupting food sources and making survival increasingly difficult.

- **Massive Flooding**: As glaciers rapidly melted, floodwaters surged into the oceans, raising sea levels and creating catastrophic **coastal inundations**. Large portions of land that had once been habitable were submerged.

- **Megafauna Extinction**: The combination of climate change and human hunting likely contributed to the extinction of large mammals like mammoths, mastodons, and saber-toothed cats. This loss of megafauna disrupted food chains, further stressing human populations who relied on these species for hunting.

Despite the severity of these changes, some groups of humans managed to survive the Younger Dryas period and its associated cataclysms. Their survival was marked by a number of key adaptations that allowed them to endure and eventually thrive in a post-flood, post-Ice Age world.

---

2. Resilience and Adaptation: The Survival Strategies of Early Humans

The survivors of the Younger Dryas and the associated floods faced significant challenges, but they also displayed remarkable resilience and ingenuity. While many early societies were impacted by climate shifts, others adapted in ways that enabled them to rebuild and progress toward the development of civilizations.

Human Adaptations to a Changing World:

- **Migration and Settlement Patterns**: As sea levels rose and floodwaters inundated fertile lands, some human groups were forced to migrate to new areas in search of resources. For example, populations in the **Near East** moved to areas of higher ground, while those in North America may have sought refuge in the **southern United States** or along river valleys.

- **Resource Diversification**: With the extinction of megafauna and the depletion of some natural resources, survivors adapted by diversifying their subsistence strategies. **Fishing, gathering**, and the cultivation of **wild plants** became increasingly important.

- **Domestication of Plants and Animals**: One of the most critical adaptations following the Younger Dryas was the development of agriculture. This shift allowed early humans to secure more stable food sources, which was essential for rebuilding society in the aftermath of the floods. The **Neolithic Revolution**—which began around **11,700 years ago**, just after the Younger Dryas—marked the transition from hunting and gathering to more permanent, agrarian lifestyles.

---

3. The Birth of Agriculture: Transitioning from Foraging to Farming

The end of the Younger Dryas coincided with a **warming climate** that brought about a more favorable environment for agriculture. The warming led to the establishment of fertile regions like the **Fertile Crescent**, where early humans began to cultivate crops and domesticate animals.

The Origins of Agriculture:

- **The Fertile Crescent**: In the Near East, the **Fertile Crescent**—a region stretching from the eastern Mediterranean through modern-day Iraq, Syria, and Iran—became the cradle of early agriculture. Archaeological evidence shows that **wheat**, **barley**, and **lentils** were among the first crops domesticated in this region, allowing human populations to establish more permanent settlements.

- **Domestication of Animals**: Along with plant domestication, humans began to tame and breed animals like **goats**, **sheep**, and **cattle**, providing reliable sources of protein, milk, and labor. The domestication of animals enabled the rise of pastoral societies and increased agricultural productivity.

- **Improved Tools and Techniques**: As humans shifted to agriculture, they developed new tools, such as **sickles** and **plows**, to help cultivate the land. This innovation allowed for larger-scale food production and the support of growing populations.

These changes did not occur uniformly around the world, but agriculture gradually spread to other regions, including **China**, **Mesoamerica**, and the **Indus Valley**, marking the beginning of agricultural societies that would lay the foundation for complex civilizations.

---

4. Social and Technological Developments: The Rise of Complex Societies

With the advent of agriculture, human societies began to organize themselves into more **complex structures**, including the development of **permanent settlements**, the establishment of **trade networks**, and the rise of **early governance systems**.

Key Developments in Post-Flood Societies:

- **Permanent Settlements**: As agriculture allowed people to stay in one place and reliably produce food, **villages** and **towns** began to emerge. Settlements grew in size and sophistication, with evidence of early **architecture, public works**, and **ritual structures**.
- **Specialization of Labor**: The surplus food generated by farming allowed for the **specialization of labor**. Some individuals focused on agricultural production, while others became skilled in crafts, construction, or trade. This diversification led to the development of **early industries** such as pottery, weaving, and metallurgy.
- **Social Hierarchies**: The growth of permanent settlements also marked the rise of **social stratification**, as individuals began to accumulate wealth and power. Early leaders emerged, and the foundations of **chieftains, tribal systems**, and eventually **kingdoms** were laid.
- **Trade Networks**: As populations grew, the exchange of goods became more complex. Early trade networks developed, facilitating the movement of goods like **obsidian, salt, textiles**, and **metal tools** across large distances.

---

5. Early Civilizations: From Survival to Thriving

By the end of the Younger Dryas, humanity had begun to recover from the worst of the **floods** and **climatic shifts**, and a number of early civilizations began to emerge. These societies were marked by advancements in **agriculture, technology**, and **social organization**.

Examples of Emerging Civilizations:

- **Sumerians and Mesopotamia**: By around **5,000 years ago**, the first great urban civilization emerged in **Mesopotamia**. The **Sumerians** in particular created the **first cities** and developed **writing** and **complex governance**. Their civilization flourished along the fertile riverbanks of the **Tigris and Euphrates**, with agriculture being central to their way of life.

- **Ancient Egypt**: Similarly, in **Egypt**, a civilization arose along the **Nile River**, relying on the annual floods of the Nile to irrigate crops and support growing urban centers. Egyptian society became one of the earliest examples of a **unified state** and achieved remarkable advancements in **architecture, mathematics**, and **engineering**.

- **The Indus Valley and China**: In the east, the **Indus Valley Civilization** flourished around the same time, with highly organized urban centers, advanced drainage systems, and trade networks. To the north, **ancient China** saw the rise of the **Xia dynasty**, marking the beginning of a long history of Chinese civilization.

6. Cultural Memory and Mythology: Remembering the Floods

Many of the cultures that arose after the Younger Dryas period retained oral traditions and myths that **remembered the catastrophic events** that shaped their ancestors' survival. **Flood myths** became a **universal theme** across different civilizations, perhaps reflecting shared memories of the traumatic flooding that accompanied the end of the Ice Age. These myths, like those in **Mesopotamia, the Bible**, and **Mesoamerica**, may have been ways to explain and cope with the deep cultural trauma left by the Younger Dryas event.

The survivors of the Younger Dryas were not just passive victims of a catastrophic event; they were active agents in rebuilding their societies and adapting to new environmental conditions. Over time, humanity transitioned from **hunter-gatherers** to **agricultural societies**, laying the groundwork for the rise of **complex civilizations**.

The resilience, innovation, and adaptation of human societies in the face of climate catastrophe stand as a testament to the **survival instincts** of early humans. As they rebuilt after the **floods** and environmental upheavals, they not only survived but thrived, creating the foundations for modern civilization. These early achievements set the stage for the cultural, technological, and societal developments that would shape the future of humanity.

Chapter 31: The Psychological Legacy of the Great Flood

Flood myths are not only foundational in understanding the cultural history of ancient societies but also provide deep insights into the **psychological and emotional responses** of early human communities to large-scale catastrophes. These myths, passed down through generations, carried within them collective memories of trauma, survival, and resilience. They reflect humanity's attempt to **make sense of the uncontrollable forces** of nature and the deep, often existential, fear of annihilation from natural disasters, while also offering a sense of hope, renewal, and transformation.

In this chapter, we explore how flood myths impacted the psychological landscape of ancient peoples, shaping their worldviews and influencing the way they interacted with their environment, with each other, and with the divine. Additionally, we look at how the transmission of these stories through generations served as a coping mechanism, reinforcing **cultural identity** and guiding future generations in times of crisis.

---

1. The Psychological Impact of Catastrophic Floods

For early human societies, the impact of sudden, catastrophic flooding would have been overwhelming. The loss of life, property, and resources would have been deeply traumatic. **Psychologically**, these kinds of events can create a **lasting fear of the uncontrollable** and the **impermanence of life**, making the human experience feel fragile and vulnerable. Early humans, living on the edge of survival in the face of such catastrophic events, would likely have experienced a profound sense of powerlessness.

Psychological Reactions to Natural Disasters:

- **Fear of Chaos and Destruction**: Flooding represents a loss of control, with water sweeping away everything in its path, eroding what humanity had worked to build. In the aftermath of the Younger Dryas and its associated floods, this fear likely drove ancient people to view floods as a symbol of cosmic chaos—a reminder that the order of the world could easily be upended.

- **Anxiety Over Divine Wrath**: In many cultures, **cataclysmic floods** were not just natural disasters but divine punishments. They were often attributed to the anger of gods or supernatural forces. The psychological impact of this belief would have been profound, instilling a sense of powerlessness before divine forces, yet also an underlying hope that such divine wrath could be appeased. This belief system may have helped communities cope with fear and uncertainty by providing a framework of religious or spiritual meaning.

- **Survival and Resilience**: Despite the overwhelming devastation, flood myths often emphasize survival and renewal. The survivors of these stories—be they **Noah**, **Utnapishtim**, or **Deucalion**—embody human **resilience**. These figures often represent hope and the ability to rebuild after destruction, providing a model for overcoming adversity. This psychological resilience can be seen as an inherent aspect of the flood myth, reinforcing the idea that even in the face of overwhelming odds, humanity can endure.

---

2. The Role of Mythology in Coping with Trauma

Mythology plays a crucial role in **cultural memory**. After a cataclysmic event such as a massive flood, societies need to make sense of what has happened, why it occurred, and how to deal with its aftermath. **Flood myths** are a way to channel collective trauma, providing an explanation for the disaster and a structure for understanding it within a **cosmic or divine framework**.

Catharsis and Moral Lessons:

- **Cathartic Release**: Flood myths provide an outlet for societies to process the emotional aftermath of disasters. The stories often include not only **devastation** but also **moral lessons**, leading to a form of **psychological catharsis**. The floods in many cultures are described as being caused by **divine punishment** for human misdeeds, and the survivors are those who have **earned favor** or been chosen by the gods. This can provide a sense of **moral order** and the belief that justice prevails even after disaster.

- **Restoration of Order**: In many myths, after the floodwaters recede, a new world order is established. This process of **rebuilding** represents the psychological need to restore a sense of balance and stability after chaos. The idea that life can return to normal after devastation offers psychological comfort, providing hope for renewal and continuity even after catastrophic loss.

Symbolism of Water and Transformation:

- **Water as a Symbol of Purification**: In many cultures, water is symbolic of both destruction and purification. It represents the cleansing of **sin** or **corruption** and the renewal of the world. The floodwaters in myths often symbolize the destruction of evil and the rebirth of a new, better world. This transformative aspect of flood myths speaks to a psychological need for **reconciliation** and **healing** after trauma.

- **Life After Death**: Flood myths also contain powerful themes of **life after death**. In some cultures, survivors of the flood are often tasked with repopulating and replenishing the earth. This echoes a deeply psychological desire for rebirth—both on a **spiritual** and a **cultural** level. The notion that humanity can begin again after such widespread devastation is profoundly optimistic and deeply ingrained in the human psyche.

---

3. The Transmission of Flood Myths: Memory and Continuity

The persistence and ubiquity of flood myths in cultures around the world point to their **psychological importance** in human societies. These myths were not just stories told for entertainment—they were a form of **cultural transmission**, carrying the collective memories of **ancestral trauma** and survival down through generations.

Cultural Memory and the Role of Oral Tradition:

- **Oral Tradition as Preservation**: Many of the ancient flood myths were transmitted orally through generations, which suggests they played an important role in preserving cultural identity. These stories became a **repository of collective memory**, allowing each generation to connect with their ancestors and their shared experiences of disaster and recovery. The repetitive nature of oral storytelling, with its ritualized recitations, also served to reinforce these memories and ensure they were passed on.

- **The Role of Storytellers**: In early societies, **storytellers** or **priests** played a significant role in transmitting these flood myths. As people shared their experiences of catastrophe and survival, storytellers would weave these accounts into narratives that could be easily remembered and retold, ensuring the flood myths remained central to cultural consciousness.

Reinforcing Identity Through Shared Trauma:

- **Solidarity and Unity**: By passing down these stories, societies could maintain a sense of **unity** and **shared identity**, even after a devastating event. The flood myths often emphasize themes of **cooperation** and **survival**, illustrating how people banded together in the face of disaster. These stories helped societies understand that they were part of something larger than themselves—part of a **community of survivors**.

- **Cultural Continuity**: The retelling of these myths also helped create a sense of **cultural continuity**, linking contemporary societies with their **ancient origins**. This continuity could serve as a psychological anchor during times of social, political, or environmental upheaval, providing reassurance that, though circumstances may change, the core of the culture—the shared myths and values—remained intact.

---

4. Flood Myths and Psychological Archetypes

Flood myths also tap into deep-seated **archetypal patterns** found within the collective unconscious, as proposed by Carl Jung. These archetypes are universal symbols and themes that appear across cultures and time periods, reflecting the core psychological experiences of humanity.

Archetypes in Flood Myths:

- **The Hero and the Savior**: In many flood myths, a central figure emerges as the **savior** or the **hero**—whether it be **Noah, Utnapishtim**, or **Deucalion**—who survives the flood and often plays a role in repopulating or renewing the world. This figure represents the **archetype of the protector** and the **renewal of hope** after destruction.

- **The Annihilation of the Old World**: The floodwaters represent the **destruction of the old world**—an archetypal cleansing of the old order. This theme can symbolize the need for **psychological renewal** after trauma. It also taps into the notion that something new can arise from destruction.

- **The Ark or Vessel**: The ark or the vessel that saves the survivors from the flood is often depicted as a **symbol of salvation**. It represents the **psychological shelter** or **container** in which the survivors are protected from the chaos outside, a kind of psychological "safe space" that preserves the seeds of future growth and development.

The psychological legacy of the great floods, as reflected in myths, is vast and profound. These stories of **destruction, resilience**, and **renewal** were not just explanations for natural phenomena, but mechanisms for understanding the **human condition**—our vulnerability, our need for hope, and our ability to adapt in the face of overwhelming odds.

Flood myths served as a tool for **psychological healing** and **cultural continuity**. They helped ancient societies make sense of **natural disasters** and the devastation they caused, offering explanations for why such events occurred and how humanity could rise from them. The **resilience** embedded within these stories shaped not only ancient societies but also influenced the psychological and cultural frameworks of subsequent generations, resonating deeply within the human psyche as a symbol of survival, transformation, and the enduring will to rebuild.

Chapter 32: The Role of Oral Tradition in Preserving Catastrophic Events

Oral traditions are one of humanity's most ancient and enduring means of preserving history, particularly in the absence of written records. These traditions, passed down through generations, are more than just storytelling; they are **cultural repositories** that carry the collective memory of societies, preserving events, values, and lessons in a form that ensures they remain integral to the identity of a community. Among the most critical aspects that oral traditions preserve are **catastrophic events**, particularly natural disasters such as floods, earthquakes, and volcanic eruptions. This chapter explores how **oral traditions helped preserve the memory of cataclysmic events** and the psychological and cultural mechanisms by which these stories helped early human societies make sense of such overwhelming occurrences.

---

1. Oral Tradition as Memory and Survival

In many ancient societies, **oral tradition** was the primary method of preserving and transmitting knowledge. Before the advent of writing, stories, histories, and cultural values were passed down through **word of mouth**—shared by **storytellers, shamans, priests**, and other members of the community. **Oral tradition** played a vital role in shaping the identity and cohesion of societies by creating a shared understanding of the world, history, and collective experiences.

The Role of Memory in Catastrophic Events:

- **Collective Memory:** Oral traditions preserved the collective memory of **catastrophic events**, helping societies make sense of their experiences and losses. In the face of major disasters, such as floods, communities relied on these stories to understand their **past**, find meaning in the devastation, and preserve the memory of their ancestors' resilience. The transmission of these memories kept the experience of the **cataclysmic event** alive, providing future generations with both a **warning** and a **lesson**.

- **Psychological Reassurance:** During times of uncertainty or trauma, oral traditions served as a psychological anchor, reassuring people that they were not alone in their suffering. The repetition of familiar flood stories provided comfort by emphasizing that **others had survived similar disasters**, giving hope to those facing their own challenges.

- **Cultural Continuity:** The transmission of stories through oral tradition also helped **preserve cultural continuity**. By ensuring that flood myths and other cataclysmic stories were passed down from one generation to the next, societies maintained a connection to their **ancestral past** and to the lessons embedded within those stories, fostering resilience and a sense of **shared identity**.

---

2. Storytelling as a Method for Making Sense of Disasters

Oral traditions were not just a way of recording events; they were a **cognitive tool** for making sense of complex and traumatic occurrences. In ancient societies, **natural disasters** were often seen as **divine interventions** or manifestations of powerful forces beyond human control. **Flood myths** and stories of other catastrophes offered a framework through which people could interpret the chaos around them, understanding it as a part of a **larger cosmic plan**.

Creating Meaning from Destruction:

- **Cosmic Order:** In many flood myths, the catastrophe is portrayed as a **divine judgment**, often as a result of **human sinfulness** or moral corruption. These stories helped explain the **cause** of the flood, turning an inexplicable disaster into a **moral lesson**. For example, the biblical **story of Noah's Ark** explains the flood as a punishment for mankind's wickedness, but also offers hope through the survival of Noah and his family, who represented **moral righteousness**.

- **Restoration of Order:** Despite the destruction, many flood myths emphasize **restoration** and **renewal**. These stories often feature survivors tasked with **rebuilding the world** and repopulating it with the knowledge, virtues, and resilience learned from the catastrophe. This cyclical theme of destruction and rebirth, embedded in oral traditions, helped people psychologically make sense of destruction, while also encouraging them to view themselves as **active agents** in the **rebirth of their societies.**

Personal and Collective Transformation:

- **Transformation through Adversity:** Cataclysmic events often catalyzed **personal and collective transformation**. In many myths, the flood serves as a kind of **rite of passage**—a trial that marks the passage from an old world to a new one. These transformations helped people cope with their own losses and fears, encouraging them to focus on **survival** and **rebuilding**.

- **Cultural Identity and Resilience:** Through oral traditions, survivors of catastrophes passed down stories that not only explained the cause of the event but also celebrated the **resilience** of the people. These tales emphasized the **human ability to endure** in the face of overwhelming odds, reinforcing **cultural identity** and ensuring that the values of perseverance and community survival were ingrained in future generations.

---

3. The Structure and Function of Flood Myths in Oral Tradition

Flood myths, as part of oral tradition, had specific structures that allowed them to function as **cultural and psychological tools**. These stories typically followed recognizable patterns that allowed listeners to connect with them more easily, reinforcing the collective memory of the **cataclysmic event** while ensuring that they could be transmitted accurately through generations.

Storytelling Techniques:

- **Repetition and Rhythm:** One of the most powerful features of oral tradition is the **repetition** of key phrases, ideas, and motifs. Repetition ensures that important themes—such as survival, divine intervention, or moral lessons—are reinforced. This technique also makes the stories easier to **remember** and **retell**. For example, the recurring themes of divine anger and salvation, as well as the journey to the ark or vessel of survival, are often repeated in similar sequences across cultures.

- **Narrative Archetypes:** Flood myths often share **common archetypal elements**, such as a divine figure or god who intervenes in human affairs, a hero or survivor who is chosen to rebuild the world, and a catastrophic event that wipes out the old world. These shared **archetypes** create a narrative structure that transcends individual cultures, allowing listeners from different societies to identify with the **universal experience of disaster** and **survival**.

- **Symbolism and Metaphor:** Flood myths often use symbolic language to convey complex emotions and societal concerns. Water in these myths symbolizes **destruction**, but it also represents **purification** and **rebirth**. The **ark** or **boat** often symbolizes **protection** and **salvation**. These symbols helped early societies make sense of the **abstract** concept of catastrophe, tying it to **concrete experiences** of survival, renewal, and human strength.

---

4. Preservation through Ritual and Community Involvement

In many cultures, the retelling of flood myths was not a passive activity—it was often tied to **rituals, festivals,** and **community gatherings**. These events served as powerful reminders of both the **trauma** of the cataclysm and the **collective resilience** in the face of adversity. By participating in these rituals, communities could **reinforce their cultural identity** and reaffirm their shared survival stories.

Rituals and Ceremonies:

- **Annual Observances:** Many ancient cultures celebrated festivals that honored the survivors of the great flood, reinforcing the myth in a cyclical manner. For example, in Mesopotamia, the **Akitu Festival** was tied to the annual renewal of kingship and the triumph of order over chaos, symbolically reflecting the themes of **rebirth** after the great deluge.

- **Community Storytelling:** Oral storytelling was often communal, with the **elder members** of society—who were seen as the **keepers of memory**—sharing the flood myths with the younger generation. This collective participation ensured that the myth became part of the **living culture**, providing continuity between generations and cementing the memory of the cataclysmic event in the **social fabric** of the community.

5. The Global Nature of Oral Traditions and Catastrophic Memories

The fact that **flood myths** are present in **virtually every culture** around the world suggests that **oral traditions** played an essential role in preserving the memory of **shared catastrophic events**. These stories are not merely anecdotal—they are likely rooted in a **real historical memory** of global floods and natural disasters that reshaped human societies thousands of years ago. This universality underscores the importance of oral tradition as a **psychological coping mechanism** and a means of maintaining **cultural continuity**.

The Global Reach of Catastrophic Memory:

- **Universal Themes**: Despite the vast diversity of cultures, the core themes of **divine judgment, survival, rebirth,** and **moral transformation** are common in flood myths worldwide. This suggests that **oral traditions** did not only preserve the **memory** of a single event but also acted as a way to understand **natural disasters** as part of the human condition, thereby linking societies from different parts of the world in their shared experience of catastrophe.

- **Cultural Diffusion**: The spread of these myths through trade, migration, and conquest helped ensure that the **collective memory** of cataclysmic events was not lost but instead continued to influence diverse civilizations across time.

Oral traditions played a critical role in preserving the memory of **catastrophic events** such as floods, earthquakes, and other natural disasters. Through **repetition, symbolism,** and **communal participation**, these stories helped societies make sense of destruction and loss, reinforcing both **cultural continuity** and the **psychological resilience** of human beings.

Flood myths, passed down through generations, have not only served as a form of **historical preservation** but also as powerful psychological and cultural tools. They helped ancient communities understand their world, survive through adversity, and rebuild after disaster, ensuring that the lessons of the past remained alive in the collective consciousness. Today, these myths continue to shape our understanding of natural disasters and our response to them, offering a timeless reminder of the human capacity for **survival, renewal,** and **hope**.

Chapter 36: The Ice Age Survivalists: Lessons from Ancient Populations

The end of the **Ice Age** and the transition into the **Holocene** were marked by dramatic environmental shifts, especially the abrupt climatic cooling associated with the **Younger Dryas** event. During this period, **prehistoric populations** faced extreme challenges—harsh cold, fluctuating climates, and changes in food availability. Despite these difficulties, human populations managed to survive, adapt, and eventually thrive as the world warmed and ecosystems shifted. This chapter explores how these **Ice Age survivalists** navigated a rapidly changing world, their **migration patterns** across the globe, and the strategies they employed to adapt and flourish.

---

1. The Harsh Realities of the Ice Age

The **Pleistocene Epoch,** which spanned from about 2.6 million years ago to 11,700 years ago, was marked by repeated **glacial cycles**. During glaciations, much of the Earth's surface was covered by massive ice sheets, and temperatures were significantly colder than they are today. This environment presented unique challenges for **prehistoric humans** and other species.

Key Environmental Challenges:

- **Extreme Cold:** Large portions of the Earth were covered by ice sheets, and temperatures were far lower than what we experience today. This cold climate made survival difficult for humans and animals alike.

- **Scarcity of Resources:** The vast ice sheets created a landscape where natural resources, particularly food sources, were limited.

Many of the megafauna species, such as mammoths, mastodons, and giant ground sloths, roamed the open tundra in search of food.

- **Fluctuating Habitats:** As glaciation advanced and retreated, the landmasses shifted, and many ecosystems changed. This created a **dynamic and unstable environment** in which humans had to constantly adapt to shifting climates, available food sources, and the distribution of animals.

Despite these harsh conditions, prehistoric populations found ways to **survive**, developing ingenious tools, social structures, and strategies that enabled them to navigate the extreme cold.

2. Human Adaptations to the Ice Age

Prehistoric humans were remarkably resourceful, employing a variety of strategies to survive the Ice Age and make use of the resources that were available to them. These strategies included innovations in technology, shelter, clothing, and hunting.

Technological Innovations:

- **Stone Tools:** Early humans relied on **stone tools** for hunting, butchering, and processing materials. Tools such as **flint spear points, scrapers**, and **blades** were essential for survival in the Ice Age, allowing humans to hunt megafauna and prepare their food in an efficient manner.

- **Fire:** Mastery over fire was a critical survival tool. Fire provided warmth, protection from predators, and the ability to cook food. It also played a key role in tool-making, as heat could be used to modify stone tools.

- **Clothing and Shelter:** The development of clothing made from animal hides was essential for surviving the frigid temperatures. Early humans used fur, leather, and woven fibers to protect themselves from the cold. They also built **shelters** using available resources, such as animal bones, wood, and stone, creating rudimentary homes that offered protection from the elements.

Hunting and Gathering:

- **Big Game Hunting:** Humans in the Ice Age were skilled hunters who relied on large game such as **mammoths**, **bison**, and **reindeer** for food, clothing, and tools. They developed sophisticated hunting strategies, including the use of **spears** and **traps**. Evidence suggests that early humans may have worked in groups to bring down large animals, using coordinated hunting tactics that involved driving herds into natural traps or over cliffs.

- **Gathering and Plant Use:** While much of the Ice Age diet was based on hunting large animals, humans also gathered **berries, roots**, and **nuts**, and later, during warmer periods, they developed more complex foraging and plant domestication strategies.

---

3. The Younger Dryas and the Disruption of Life

The **Younger Dryas** was a period of dramatic cooling that lasted from about 12,900 to 11,700 years ago. This event abruptly interrupted the warming trend that had followed the last Ice Age and led to a significant **climate crisis**. Temperatures in the Northern Hemisphere plunged, causing environmental conditions to worsen.

Impact on Mega-fauna and Human Populations:

- **Extinction of Megafauna:** One of the most profound impacts of the Younger Dryas was the **extinction of many megafauna species**, including mammoths, mastodons, and saber-toothed tigers. These large animals were unable to adapt to the colder conditions, and their loss significantly altered the food chain and ecosystems.

- **Human Adaptation:** Early humans had to adapt quickly to these shifts. With the disappearance of large game, hunter-gatherer societies had to innovate new strategies. This likely led to a greater focus on smaller game and the development of **fishing techniques** and more diverse plant use. The crisis also could have fostered new forms of **social cooperation**, as groups banded together to tackle the challenges of surviving in a harsher, more unpredictable climate.

The Younger Dryas event is believed to have been a catalyst for **cultural change** in prehistoric populations, including the development of **agriculture** in some areas, as people sought more stable food sources.

4. Migration Patterns During and After the Younger Dryas

As the climate shifted during the Younger Dryas, human populations had to respond to environmental pressures by **migrating** to more hospitable areas. These migrations helped shape the demographic distribution of early human societies.

Northward and Southward Migrations:

- **Migration Out of Africa:** The end of the Ice Age marked the culmination of the **Out of Africa** migration. Early humans had already spread across the continents, but the **end of the Ice Age** and the subsequent climatic shifts encouraged further movement. Populations moved into previously uninhabited regions, adapting to new environments and creating new cultural landscapes.

- **Bering Land Bridge and the Americas:** One of the most significant migrations during this period was the movement of humans into the **Americas**. It is widely believed that early humans crossed the **Bering Land Bridge**, which connected Siberia to Alaska, around the end of the Ice Age. Evidence of **Clovis culture** in North America suggests that these migrants had sophisticated hunting technologies and were capable of thriving in the challenging environments of the New World.

- **Southern Migrations:** While many populations moved into cooler northern areas or the Americas, some groups migrated south into **warmer regions**, seeking stable food sources in areas that remained unaffected by the ice sheets. These populations adapted to new environments, developing new cultural practices and forms of subsistence.

Climate Change and Settling Patterns:

- As the Younger Dryas ended and the Earth warmed into the **Holocene**, ecosystems gradually became more hospitable. The warmer temperatures allowed for the **growth of forests**, the spread of **grasslands**, and the eventual rise of **agriculture** in many parts of the world. Humans who had once relied on hunting and gathering began to settle in fertile areas, cultivating crops and domesticating animals.

5. Lessons from the Ice Age Survivalists

The ability of prehistoric populations to survive during the Ice Age and adapt to the sudden climatic changes of the Younger Dryas holds critical lessons for us today, especially in the context of **climate change** and **environmental adaptation**.

Adaptation and Innovation:

- Prehistoric humans demonstrated incredible **resilience** and **resourcefulness** in the face of extreme challenges. Their ability to innovate new technologies, adapt to changing environments, and develop social strategies for survival laid the foundation for modern human societies.
- Today, as the world faces its own environmental and climatic challenges, there is much to learn from how early humans coped with a dramatically changing world. The lessons from the Ice Age survivalists emphasize the importance of **flexibility**, **innovation**, and **cooperation** in navigating **global crises**.

Migration and Resilience:

- The migration patterns of ancient humans highlight the capacity for human populations to **move**, adapt, and settle in new areas in response to climate-induced pressures. In our increasingly interconnected world, we must be mindful of the role that migration plays in the survival of human societies during times of **climate stress** and **resource scarcity**.
- The resilience shown by ancient populations can inspire modern communities to adapt to current challenges, be it environmental, social, or economic.

The story of the Ice Age survivalists is one of profound **adaptation** and **resilience**. Despite the harshest of conditions, prehistoric humans found ways to survive and thrive through technological innovation, social cooperation, and cultural resilience. As we face our own environmental challenges in the modern world, the experiences of these early humans offer valuable insights into the **power of human ingenuity** and the importance of adapting to ever-changing climates. By studying their migration patterns, survival strategies, and cultural practices, we can better understand how to navigate our own rapidly changing world.

Chapter 44: The Role of Myth in Explaining Natural Disasters

Throughout history, **natural disasters**—whether floods, earthquakes, droughts, or volcanic eruptions—have been experienced by countless civilizations across the globe. When faced with these cataclysmic events, ancient societies lacked the scientific knowledge to explain their causes, leading them to turn to **mythology** as a framework for understanding and interpreting such phenomena. Flood myths, in particular, have appeared in virtually every culture, often as a central element in their **creation stories**, **moral lessons**, and **cosmological beliefs**. These myths not only provided explanations for the devastating consequences of natural disasters but also helped people cope with and make sense of an unpredictable and dangerous world.

In this chapter, we will delve into the role of myth, specifically **flood myths**, in explaining natural disasters across the globe. We will explore how these myths reflect the environmental changes experienced by different cultures, their underlying themes, and the ways in which they sought to **understand and explain** the forces of nature.

---

1. The Role of Myth in Early Human Understanding

Before the advent of scientific inquiry and the development of **geology**, **meteorology**, or other branches of knowledge, people relied on **stories and myths** to make sense of their experiences. These myths were not just tales of gods and heroes but were rooted in the practical and emotional realities of **survival** in a world governed by **natural forces**. Floods, in particular, stood out as one of the most destructive and transformative disasters, often reshaping the landscape, displacing communities, and threatening survival.

The Function of Myths in Ancient Societies:

- **Explanation of the Unexplainable:** Without the tools of modern science, floods and other natural disasters seemed to come from nowhere and could often seem like random and unfair acts of nature. Myths provided **cosmological frameworks** that tied these disasters to divine will or **cosmic order**, offering an explanation for why such events occurred and what they meant for human beings.

- **Cultural Identity and Continuity:** Myths are key to maintaining **cultural identity** and preserving shared values. They offered narratives of **survival**, resilience, and **rebirth** that helped communities cope with the trauma of floods and other disasters. They became a **collective memory** of catastrophe, passed down through generations to explain the world and the relationship between humans, nature, and the divine.

- **Moral and Social Lessons:** Many flood myths were not just about natural disasters but were also morality tales that reflected the values and beliefs of the society. They were a means of teaching important lessons about human behavior, such as the consequences of **hubris, greed,** or **immorality**. Floods were often seen as divine retribution for human wrongdoing or a means of cleansing the earth to restore balance.

---

2. Common Themes in Flood Myths Across Cultures

Flood myths are a ubiquitous feature in world mythology, with similarities often emerging across cultures that were geographically and temporally separated. These common themes provide insight into how different societies viewed their relationship with nature and the divine. Here are several themes that appear across flood myths:

Divine Retribution and Cleansing:

- Many cultures view floods as the **wrath of the gods** or a necessary act to cleanse the world of human **corruption** and **evil**. In these myths, the flood is a form of **divine punishment**, where only a few righteous or chosen individuals survive, signaling the triumph of **virtue** over **sin**.

- In the **Sumerian Epic of Gilgamesh**, the gods send a flood to wipe out humanity, which they view as too noisy and bothersome. Similarly, in the **Bible**, the flood in the story of Noah is a result of God's judgment upon the wickedness of humanity.

Survival and Rebirth:

- Flood myths often depict a scenario where a select few survivors—often **heroes, deities,** or **moral exemplars**—are chosen to survive and repopulate the earth after the waters subside. These figures are often provided with a boat, ark, or other vessel that shields them from the floodwaters. Their survival signifies the possibility of **rebirth, renewal**, and the creation of a new world order.

- In the **Noah's Ark** story, Noah and his family are spared by God's intervention, and they go on to repopulate the Earth, thus beginning a new era. Similarly, in the **Mayan myth**, the gods send a flood to rid the world of humans, but the **surviving hero twins** are tasked with recreating humanity.

A Cosmic Reset:

- The flood in many myths is seen as a **cosmic reset**, a necessary event to **restore balance** to a world that had gone astray. This theme reflects the cyclical nature of the earth's existence—periods of creation and destruction, flourishing and decay.

- In the **Greek myth** of **Deucalion and Pyrrha**, the flood is a cleansing event intended to rid the Earth of the **impious**, but afterward, the survivors are instructed to throw stones behind them to create a new human race, symbolizing the concept of renewal.

---

3. The Psychological Function of Flood Myths

Flood myths serve an important **psychological role** for societies experiencing natural disasters. The overwhelming power and destruction of floods can cause deep feelings of helplessness, fear, and loss. By providing a **mythological explanation**, these stories helped people make sense of these chaotic events and offer **comfort** and **hope**.

Coping with Catastrophe:

- Myths allow communities to **process trauma** and make sense of the devastating effects of floods. By framing these events within a narrative structure that includes **moral lessons** and **divine intervention**, ancient peoples could **reconcile** the experience of disaster with a sense of meaning and order.
- The survival of certain individuals or families within flood myths serves as a metaphor for **resilience** and **hope**. These stories remind societies that even in the face of overwhelming destruction, life can be renewed, and communities can rebuild.

Transmission of Wisdom:

- The transmission of flood myths through **oral tradition** helped communities remember the devastation of the past and **prepare for the future**. These stories preserved the collective memory of natural disasters, allowing future generations to learn from the experiences of their ancestors.
- In many cases, flood myths contained **practical wisdom**, such as knowledge of **flood-prone areas**, the importance of **land management**, or strategies for coping with severe weather conditions. These myths thus became a vital component of **survival knowledge**.

---

4. Environmental and Geological Insights in Myth

Interestingly, many flood myths contain **geological and environmental elements** that resonate with the experiences of ancient peoples living through significant **climatic events**. While the mythological interpretations often have religious or symbolic significance, they may also reflect real-world events and natural phenomena.

Global Flood Events and Regional Myths:

- Geological evidence suggests that many ancient cultures experienced **cataclysmic floods**, likely caused by **glacial meltwater** or sudden **sea-level rise**. In some cases, these events may have been localized, but in others, the scale of the flooding could have been much larger. It is plausible that these actual historical floods became **mythologized** over time, becoming stories of divine wrath or cosmic resets.

- For example, the **Black Sea flood hypothesis** suggests that the inundation of the Black Sea basin around 5,600 BCE may have inspired flood myths in **Mesopotamian, Greek**, and **Turkish** traditions. Similarly, the flooding caused by the melting of **glacial lakes** at the end of the Ice Age could have influenced the flood narratives of the **Americas** and **Europe**.

Symbolism of Water:

- Water in flood myths is often symbolic of **life, death**, and **renewal**. The floodwaters are seen as a destructive force, but they also cleanse the earth and create the possibility for new beginnings. This dual symbolism reflects humanity's **relationship** with water as both a life-giving and potentially destructive force.

- In some myths, the flood itself is portrayed as **necessary** for the survival of future generations, showing the symbolic importance of water as a dynamic force of both creation and destruction.

Flood myths from around the world provide a fascinating glimpse into how **ancient peoples** tried to make sense of **natural disasters**. These myths served not only as religious narratives but as essential frameworks for understanding the **forces of nature** that shaped human life and survival. The themes of **divine retribution, cosmic renewal**, and **moral lessons** remain central to these stories, as they offer a lens through which humans could understand and **cope with the unpredictable** nature of the world.

While **modern science** has provided us with explanations for many natural disasters, flood myths continue to resonate with us because they encapsulate universal human themes of **survival, resilience**, and **renewal**. The myths remain an enduring testament to humanity's enduring effort to make sense of the world and our place within it, offering valuable lessons for us as we confront the environmental challenges of our time.

Part VI: The Flood Myth Legacy in Modern Times

Chapter 50: Modern Interpretations of the Younger Dryas Impact

The **Younger Dryas** is a period of abrupt and dramatic climate change that occurred around **12,900 years ago**, marking a sudden return to cold conditions after the gradual warming of the Earth following the last Ice Age. This event not only caused significant shifts in global climate but is also tied to large-scale extinction events, notably the extinction of **megafauna** and the disruption of human cultures such as the **Clovis culture** in North America. While scientists once attributed this cooling to gradual changes in Earth's climate systems, contemporary research has increasingly pointed to the possibility of a **cosmic impact**, such as a comet or asteroid strike, as a contributing factor to this climatic anomaly.

The modern interpretation of the **Younger Dryas impact hypothesis** suggests that a comet or asteroid, or a series of smaller objects, could have triggered a **cataclysmic series of events** leading to the rapid climate shift. This theory has gained attention due to new evidence in the form of **geological markers**, **chemical traces**, and **archaeological findings** that indicate something extraordinary occurred at the boundary of the Younger Dryas.

This chapter will explore how contemporary scientists interpret the Younger Dryas, its connection to the impact hypothesis, and how these modern ideas intersect with our understanding of **climate change**, **extinction events**, and the broader implications for **planetary vulnerability**.

---

1. The Younger Dryas Cooling: A Rapid and Dramatic Change

Before exploring the modern interpretations, it's important to establish the characteristics of the Younger Dryas event. This period occurred around 12,900 years ago and lasted about 1,200 years. During this time, temperatures in the Northern Hemisphere plunged dramatically, reversing the warming that had been happening as Earth emerged from the last Ice Age. The cooling during the Younger Dryas is considered one of the most abrupt climate shifts in the **Holocene** and likely had widespread effects on both the environment and the species living during that time.

- **The Impact on Climate:** The most striking feature of the Younger Dryas was the sudden and severe cooling, which led to significant environmental disruption. Ice sheets in the northern latitudes expanded again, and **temperature drops** in the **Arctic** and **Europe** were as much as 10-15°C within just a few decades.

- **Biological and Ecological Impact:** The cooling likely caused widespread disruption to ecosystems, including the decline of the **megafauna** (e.g., mammoths, mastodons, saber-toothed tigers), as well as shifts in vegetation patterns. Many large species were unable to adapt to the rapid climate change, contributing to their eventual extinction.

- **Human Impact:** The cooling period coincided with the demise of the **Clovis culture**, one of the first widespread human cultures in North America. This sudden climatic shift may have caused **food shortages** and **population displacement**, further contributing to the decline of the Clovis people.

2. The Younger Dryas Impact Hypothesis

In recent decades, the **Younger Dryas Impact Hypothesis** has gained traction as a potential explanation for the abrupt climate change that occurred during this period. This hypothesis posits that a **cosmic object**, likely a **comet** or **asteroid**, struck the Earth around 12,900 years ago, releasing an immense amount of energy and triggering a cascade of catastrophic events, including wildfires, the release of **carbon aerosols**, and disruptions to the Earth's climate systems.

The **impact hypothesis** originated from observations of unusual **geological markers** and evidence of **extraterrestrial materials** found in sediment layers dating to the Younger Dryas boundary. Researchers, including **Richard Firestone**, **Allen West**, and **Simon L. G. Lewis**, have argued that this event might explain the sudden cooling and ecological shifts observed during this period.

Key Evidence Supporting the Impact Hypothesis:

1. **Nanodiamonds:** One of the strongest pieces of evidence for the Younger Dryas Impact Hypothesis is the discovery of **nanodiamonds**

in sediment layers from this time period. These **microscopic diamonds** are formed under extreme pressure, such as that generated by a **cosmic impact**. The presence of these nanodiamonds at multiple sites around the world suggests that an impact event occurred at or around the Younger Dryas boundary.

2. **Iridium and Platinum Anomalies: Iridium** and **platinum**, metals often associated with extraterrestrial objects like asteroids or comets, have been found in high concentrations in the sediment layers corresponding to the Younger Dryas. Iridium, in particular, is rare on Earth but is found in larger quantities in asteroids, making its presence in the geological record significant evidence for a cosmic impact.

3. **Charcoal and Evidence of Wildfires:** Evidence of widespread **wildfires** is found in the same layers that show signs of the Younger Dryas impact. **Charcoal deposits** and **soot** from fires have been discovered in these sediments, suggesting that the impact caused massive fires across large areas of the Earth's surface. This would have released large quantities of **carbon** into the atmosphere, contributing to the climate cooling by blocking sunlight.

4. **Shocked Quartz and Tektites: Shocked quartz**, a form of quartz that is altered by the intense pressure generated by high-energy impacts, has been found in sediments from the Younger Dryas period. Additionally, **tektites**, which are glassy fragments formed by the melting of rock during impacts, have also been discovered. Both of these materials are consistent with the aftermath of a **high-energy extraterrestrial impact**.

---

3. The Broader Impact of the Younger Dryas Event on Climate and Extinctions

The catastrophic events associated with the Younger Dryas impact, including the cooling of the climate and the occurrence of widespread wildfires, may have led to significant changes in the Earth's environment and ecosystems. These changes likely triggered **extinction events** and profound shifts in the balance of ecosystems.

- **Megafauna Extinction:** The most notable consequence of the Younger Dryas cooling was the **extinction of megafauna** such as mammoths, mastodons, and saber-toothed cats. The cooling and ecological disruption caused by the impact likely contributed to the disappearance of many large species, which were already struggling due to **overhunting** by human populations.

- **Human Populations:** The sudden climate cooling would have placed considerable stress on human populations, particularly in the Americas, where the **Clovis culture** had already been thriving. The **disappearance of megafauna** and the disruptions to ecosystems may have led to food shortages, forcing human populations to adapt by changing their hunting and gathering strategies.

- **Ocean Circulation and the "Freshwater Event":** The impact may also have triggered **massive freshwater floods**, disrupting the Earth's **ocean circulation systems**. This event, which may have involved the release of **meltwater** from glacial lakes, could have contributed to the cooling by affecting the **Atlantic Meridional Overturning Circulation** (AMOC), which regulates the Earth's climate.

---

4. Connections to Modern Theories of Climate Change and Extinction Events

While the **Younger Dryas Impact Hypothesis** is still debated within the scientific community, it has important implications for our understanding of both **climate change** and **extinction events** in Earth's history, and it provides important context for modern theories about the role of **catastrophes** in shaping the planet's environment.

The Role of Extraterrestrial Impacts in Climate and Extinction:

- The hypothesis that cosmic impacts can trigger dramatic shifts in climate resonates with modern concerns about the potential for **asteroid** and **comet impacts** to influence Earth's environment in the present and future. Understanding past impacts, such as the Younger Dryas, helps scientists better prepare for the possibility of similar events in the future, which could lead to **global climate change** and the **extinction of species**.

Climate Change and Feedback Loops:

- The Younger Dryas cooling provides a **model for abrupt climate change**, showing that Earth's climate can shift dramatically and rapidly due to both **extraterrestrial** and **terrestrial factors**. This offers important lessons for modern climate change models, which often focus on gradual warming due to human activities like **greenhouse gas emissions**. The possibility of sudden, catastrophic changes—whether due to natural causes like impacts or human-induced factors—remains an important consideration for future climate projections.

5. Criticisms and Alternatives to the Impact Hypothesis

Despite the growing body of evidence for the Younger Dryas impact theory, there are critics who argue that alternative explanations may be more plausible.

- **Volcanic Activity:** Some scientists propose that large-scale **volcanic eruptions** could have contributed to the cooling by releasing vast amounts of **sulfur** into the atmosphere, which would have blocked sunlight and cooled the planet.

- **Ocean Circulation Changes:** Other theories suggest that the abrupt cooling was due to shifts in ocean circulation, particularly the disruption of the **Atlantic Meridional Overturning Circulation (AMOC)**, which could have been triggered by the sudden influx of **meltwater** from the retreating ice sheets.

Modern interpretations of the Younger Dryas impact hypothesis shed light on the potential role of **extraterrestrial events** in shaping Earth's climate and ecosystems. The possibility that a comet or asteroid strike caused an abrupt and catastrophic climate event has significant implications for our understanding of extinction events and climate change. Whether or not the

Younger Dryas impact hypothesis is ultimately confirmed, the research surrounding it underscores the importance of **studying catastrophic events** in Earth's past to better understand how our planet's environment can be altered by natural phenomena—and how future **humanity** might adapt to such challenges.

Chapter 57: Flood Myths and Environmental Awareness

Flood myths are among the most widespread and enduring stories found across various cultures, often depicting catastrophic deluges that reshape the world. From the Biblical **Noah's Ark** to the **Mesopotamian** tale of **Utnapishtim**, these myths have persisted through generations, shaping the cultural consciousness about natural disasters, human survival, and the relationship between humanity and the environment.

In the contemporary world, where the impacts of **climate change**, rising **sea levels**, and **global warming** are becoming increasingly urgent, flood myths take on a new significance. These ancient stories can offer insights into humanity's early understandings of **environmental change**, and they continue to resonate in modern discussions about **ecological balance** and **environmental stewardship**.

This chapter will explore how flood myths are more than just ancient tales—they are powerful cultural tools that can help shape **modern environmental consciousness**. We will also investigate how the symbolic elements of flood myths reflect humanity's long-standing awareness of the **fragility of life** and the **vulnerability of civilizations** to environmental upheaval.

---

1. The Role of Flood Myths in Ancient Cultures

Flood myths appear in nearly every culture across the world, often centered on similar themes: divine punishment, renewal, destruction, and rebirth. These narratives typically feature a **great flood** that wipes out civilization, with only a select few survivors or a single family escaping to repopulate the Earth. But beyond their mythological significance, these stories hold deeper meanings about human-environment interactions.

Common Themes in Flood Myths:

- **Punishment and Rebirth**: In many myths, floods serve as a punishment for human hubris or moral failings, but they also pave the way for a new beginning. The **Noah's Ark** story, for example, involves divine retribution for human corruption, followed by the promise of renewal.

- **Survival and Resilience**: The survivors of these floods often embody **resilience** and **adaptability** in the face of catastrophe, echoing the enduring human capacity to survive natural disasters.

- **Humanity's Relationship with Nature**: Many flood myths also underline the precarious balance between humanity and the natural world. The flood becomes a metaphor for how human actions, particularly in relation to **nature's cycles**, can bring about both creation and destruction.

These common themes reflect ancient cultures' recognition of **nature's power** and their understanding that human survival depended on a **careful relationship** with the environment. Flood myths function as warnings about the dangers of **environmental degradation** or the **overstepping of natural boundaries**.

---

2. Flood Myths and Modern Environmental Concerns

In the 21st century, the environmental significance of flood myths is more relevant than ever. With rising concerns about **climate change**, **global warming**, and **natural disasters**, these ancient stories offer rich metaphors for the ecological crises we face today.

Climate Change and Rising Sea Levels

- As global temperatures rise, **sea levels** are also rising, threatening coastal communities and low-lying islands around the world. This phenomenon evokes ancient flood myths in the sense that they remind humanity of the destructive potential of water and the fragility of human settlements in the face of nature's power.

Modern scientists warn that if **global warming** continues unchecked, flooding could become one of the most devastating impacts of climate change, especially in **vulnerable regions** like the **Pacific Islands**, **Bangladesh**, and **Florida's coastline**. Flood myths from places like the

Polynesian islands and **the Americas** offer powerful metaphors for understanding the relationship between human civilization and water.

Ecosystem Destruction and Biodiversity Loss

- The idea of a **flood as destruction** can also symbolize the ongoing damage to the Earth's ecosystems, driven by **deforestation, pollution,** and **unsustainable agricultural practices**. Just as the floodwaters in ancient myths wash away corrupt or unsustainable human systems, modern environmentalists see an impending flood-like event in the form of **mass extinction** and **biodiversity loss**. These floods are not just literal, but also metaphorical representations of the consequences of **environmental mismanagement**.

The idea of **rebirth** in flood myths—especially in stories where survivors rebuild from the ruins—echoes the environmentalist hope that humanity can learn from its mistakes and restore the planet before it is too late.

---

3. Flood Myths as Ecological Warnings

Flood myths can also function as **warnings** about the consequences of **environmental neglect**. They serve as a cultural mechanism for passing down knowledge about the natural world, **respecting limits**, and understanding the inevitable repercussions of **overexploitation**.

Respecting Nature's Limits

- Flood myths frequently emphasize humanity's **failure** to live in harmony with nature, leading to divine retribution or catastrophe. These tales speak to humanity's growing **disregard** for the environment, and they highlight the need for responsible resource management and **environmental stewardship**.

For example, in the **Babylonian flood myth** of **Atrahasis**, humanity's overpopulation and overconsumption of resources anger the gods, resulting in a great flood that wipes out most of humanity. This myth parallels modern concerns about **overpopulation, overconsumption,** and **resource depletion**, providing a timeless reminder of how unchecked growth can have dire consequences.

Balance and Harmony

- Many ancient flood myths also speak to the importance of **balance** between human societies and the environment. The **Mayan** flood myth, for instance, conveys themes of **hubris** and the need for human beings to recognize their place within the broader natural order. Today, environmental advocates emphasize similar ideas of balance, calling for **sustainable practices** that respect both human needs and the limits of Earth's ecosystems.

---

4. The Legacy of Flood Myths in Environmental Movements

Flood myths have long been used to promote environmental awareness, even inspiring some of the key ideas behind **modern conservation** and **ecology**.

Spiritual and Moral Foundations

- The **moral** and **spiritual** lessons embedded in these myths continue to inspire **eco-consciousness** today. For instance, the idea of a **global flood** symbolizes humanity's collective responsibility to care for the Earth and future generations. The belief that humanity must avoid exploiting natural resources recklessly mirrors the need to curb **unsustainable agricultural practices, overfishing**, and **deforestation** that are contributing to the degradation of the planet.

- **Cultural Identity and Environmental Justice**: Many communities, particularly indigenous groups, continue to view flood myths as central to their cultural identity and their **relationship with nature**. In these communities, **environmental justice movements** often draw on flood myth narratives to highlight the need for **environmental protection**, especially in the face of climate change. The myth of the flood serves as a rallying cry for the preservation of ancestral lands, sustainable living, and the safeguarding of vital ecosystems.

---

5. The Role of Flood Myths in Contemporary Environmental Action

As global awareness of **climate change** and **global warming** grows, flood myths are being invoked in a variety of contexts to raise awareness and galvanize action. They are increasingly used in **documentaries, art, literature,** and **education** to convey the urgency of **environmental protection** and the need to address climate-related risks.

Modern Adaptations and Awareness Campaigns

- Many modern environmental campaigns, such as those advocating for the reduction of **carbon emissions, climate change adaptation,** and the preservation of **wetlands**, are influenced by the same ethical and moral lessons contained in flood myths. **Flood myths**, with their messages of **rebirth, renewal,** and the **cycle of destruction**, are used as potent symbols in these campaigns, calling for a balance between the human need for progress and the imperative to **protect the environment.**

Education and Reflection

- Educational programs for children and adults increasingly use these myths to foster **environmental stewardship**. By linking ancient wisdom with modern scientific understanding of **climate change**, flood myths offer both a **reflection on the past** and a **warning for the future**, reminding people of the fragility of the world we inhabit and the importance of living in harmony with nature.

Flood myths, though ancient, retain significant relevance today as we face the growing challenges of **climate change, rising sea levels,** and **ecological collapse**. These stories offer a **powerful lens** through which we can understand humanity's role in **nature** and our relationship with the planet. They remind us of the **vulnerability** of civilizations in the face of **natural forces** and the consequences of **disregarding environmental balance**.

Ultimately, the enduring power of flood myths lies not only in their historical significance but in their continued relevance in shaping modern attitudes toward **environmental stewardship**. By reflecting on these myths, we can learn valuable lessons about the importance of **respecting the Earth**, working towards **sustainability**, and ensuring that we, as a species, do not repeat the mistakes of the past.

Chapter 60: The Younger Dryas and the Search for Lost Civilizations

The Younger Dryas period, a mysterious and abrupt cold spell that lasted from approximately 12,900 to 11,700 years ago, marks one of the most significant climate shifts in Earth's history. This sudden climatic reversal, believed to have been triggered by a cosmic event, left lasting impacts on the planet's ecosystems, climate, and human civilizations. The end of the Ice Age and the dramatic climate changes during the Younger Dryas may have caused massive disruptions for early human cultures, some of which could have led to the destruction of ancient civilizations—perhaps even civilizations lost to time and myth.

One of the most enduring ideas surrounding this catastrophic event is the search for **lost civilizations**—particularly the legendary **Atlantis** or other forgotten cultures that may have existed before the Younger Dryas impact. This chapter delves into the intriguing possibility that the dramatic shifts brought about by the Younger Dryas could have contributed to the collapse of advanced ancient cultures. The search for these lost civilizations continues to spark both scientific and speculative inquiry, blurring the lines between myth, history, and archaeology.

---

1. The Younger Dryas: A Global Catastrophe

Before delving into the search for lost civilizations, it's essential to understand the scope of the **Younger Dryas** event. Around 12,900 years ago, Earth experienced an abrupt and extreme cooling, lasting for approximately 1,200 years. Temperatures that had been warming at the close of the Ice Age suddenly dropped, plunging much of the Northern Hemisphere back into near-glacial conditions. This cooling is thought to have been caused by an enormous influx of **freshwater** into the Atlantic Ocean, disrupting the **Atlantic Meridional Overturning Circulation (AMOC)**, which helped regulate global temperatures.

There are several key effects of the Younger Dryas that could have influenced the development of ancient civilizations:

- **Climate Instability**: The sudden return to cold and dry conditions would have severely impacted agricultural development, which was already in its infancy during this period. Crops would have failed, and regions that were once hospitable became inhospitable.

- **Megafauna Extinctions**: Many of the large animals (mammoths, mastodons, and saber-toothed cats) that humans relied on for food and resources went extinct during the Younger Dryas. This could have severely affected human populations that depended on hunting megafauna.

- **Displacement and Migration**: The harsh climatic conditions likely led to the mass migration of human populations. These migrations, combined with the loss of natural resources, could have led to the collapse of established communities and the formation of new ones in more hospitable regions.

Given the widespread and sudden nature of these disruptions, some theories suggest that **advanced civilizations** existed before this time and were wiped out by the catastrophic changes of the Younger Dryas. The search for these lost civilizations, such as the myth of **Atlantis**, is intertwined with attempts to understand the scope and impact of this ancient catastrophe.

---

2. The Legend of Atlantis: A Civilization Destroyed by Catastrophe

The most famous lost civilization in human history is **Atlantis**, a mythic landmass described by the ancient Greek philosopher **Plato** in his dialogues, *Timaeus* and *Critias*. Plato's account, written around 360 BCE, describes Atlantis as a powerful and technologically advanced civilization located beyond the "Pillars of Hercules" (the Strait of Gibraltar). The Atlanteans were said to possess immense wealth, knowledge, and military power, but their arrogance and greed led to their downfall. According to Plato, Atlantis was eventually submerged into the sea as a result of a **great catastrophe**.

While the existence of Atlantis remains debated and widely regarded as myth, some researchers believe that Plato's story may be based on **real historical events**, such as the destruction of a pre-existing civilization due to a catastrophic natural disaster. This theory often connects Atlantis with the Younger Dryas, suggesting that the lost civilization Plato described could have been wiped out by the abrupt climate change and global disruptions that occurred during the Younger Dryas.

The Connection to the Younger Dryas:

- **The Catastrophic Event**: Some believe that Atlantis was destroyed by a catastrophic flood or seismic event caused by the massive changes in Earth's climate at the time. If the Younger Dryas impact hypothesis is correct, a **cosmic impact** could have triggered massive floods, tsunamis, and earthquakes, which could have decimated civilizations around the world.

- **The Submergence of Land**: The idea that Atlantis was submerged by the sea has been interpreted in the context of **rising sea levels** after the Younger Dryas. The rapid **meltwater pulses** from melting glaciers could have caused significant shifts in sea levels, flooding coastal regions and wiping out low-lying civilizations. This could be the basis for the Atlantis myth of a lost land submerged beneath the ocean.

Though there is no direct archaeological evidence linking the Younger Dryas to Atlantis, the possibility of a cataclysmic event that led to the destruction of a lost civilization has spurred ongoing searches for Atlantis in locations such as the **Azores**, the **Caribbean**, and the **Mediterranean**.

---

3. Other Lost Civilizations: The Search for Pre-Younger Dryas Cultures

Beyond Atlantis, the Younger Dryas has also fueled speculation about other lost civilizations—advanced cultures that could have existed before the Ice Age catastrophe and were subsequently wiped out. These cultures are often described in mythological terms but have also been the subject of archaeological and speculative investigation.

Göbekli Tepe: The World's Oldest Temple Complex

One of the most compelling examples of pre-Ice Age civilizations is **Göbekli Tepe**, an ancient archaeological site located in present-day Turkey. Estimated to be around **12,000 years old**, Göbekli Tepe predates known civilizations by several millennia, and its complex megalithic structures challenge the conventional understanding of early human societies.

Some researchers believe that **Göbekli Tepe** could be the remnants of a **pre-Younger Dryas** civilization that was destroyed or abandoned in the aftermath of the catastrophic climate change. Its construction might have been halted or disrupted by the environmental upheaval associated with the Younger Dryas, possibly leading to the loss of advanced knowledge and techniques.

The Megalithic Sites of Europe and the Americas

Other examples of potential pre-Ice Age civilizations include the megalithic structures found in **Europe**, such as the **Stonehenge** complex in England and **Carnac** in France, as well as the ancient ruins of the **Maya** and **Inca** in the Americas. Though these sites are generally thought to have been constructed in the post-Ice Age period, some theories suggest that these civilizations might have inherited knowledge from even older cultures that were wiped out during the Younger Dryas.

Theoretical Links to the Younger Dryas

- These civilizations could have been the inheritors of **older technologies** and cultures that were destroyed during the abrupt climatic shift of the Younger Dryas. As populations migrated in search of stable environments, they could have carried remnants of their knowledge with them, eventually giving rise to the advanced civilizations that followed.

---

4. The Role of Myth in Preserving Memories of Lost Civilizations

Myths about **lost civilizations** are often seen as cultural memories passed down through generations, reflecting real events that occurred in the distant past. These myths may have been shaped by the traumatic experiences of early human societies, who lived through catastrophic events like the Younger Dryas. Such myths would be the stories of survivors—the descendants of those who endured environmental upheavals, displacement, and the destruction of their cities.

The enduring nature of stories like **Atlantis** or the **flood myths** in the Americas, Asia, and Europe may be the result of this collective memory, with each culture interpreting these events through its own lens. The myth of **Atlantis**, for example, could be a metaphor for the survivors of a much older civilization who passed down their history through stories.

---

5. Modern Investigations and the Search for Lost Civilizations

In modern times, researchers continue to explore the possibility that civilizations existed before the Younger Dryas but were lost due to the events of the time. The search for evidence of such civilizations often involves the exploration of submerged sites, ancient ruins, and mysterious artifacts that may provide clues to the existence of pre-Ice Age cultures.

- **Submerged Cities**: Advances in underwater archaeology have led to the discovery of ancient cities submerged off the coast of **India**, **Japan**, and the **Caribbean**. Some of these sites, such as the underwater ruins near the coast of **Cuba** and the **Bimini Road** in the Bahamas, have fueled speculation that they could be remnants of ancient civilizations wiped out by the sea-level rise associated with the Younger Dryas.

- **Archaeological Anomalies**: Discoveries of ancient structures, tools, and artifacts that suggest advanced technology predating the commonly accepted timeline of human history continue to intrigue archaeologists. Sites like **Gobekli Tepe**, the **Piri Reis map**, and various **megalithic structures** support the notion that human civilizations might have reached an advanced state far earlier than traditionally believed.

The Younger Dryas is not only a turning point in the Earth's climate but also a pivotal moment in the history of human civilization. Whether or not ancient civilizations existed before this cataclysmic event remains a subject of debate, but the evidence suggests that the Younger Dryas could have played a central role in reshaping human history. As the search for lost civilizations continues, the search for connections between these ancient cultures and the catastrophe of the Younger Dryas reminds us that the past is often more complex than we realize—and that the stories we tell today may carry echoes of a much older world.

Chapter 64: The Role of the Flood Myth in Popular Culture

Flood myths, with their deeply ingrained themes of destruction, survival, and rebirth, have found their way into a broad array of **popular culture**. From movies and television shows to books and video games, the themes of cataclysmic floods and the subsequent rebuilding of civilization resonate with audiences worldwide. These myths, rooted in ancient traditions, continue to serve as potent symbols in storytelling, often embodying the tension between human fragility and resilience in the face of overwhelming natural forces.

In this chapter, we explore the ways in which **flood myths** have been integrated into **modern media**, reflecting both timeless human concerns about the environment and the existential questions about humanity's place in a constantly changing world. By examining examples from film, literature, and other forms of popular culture, we can understand how these myths continue to shape contemporary narratives and provoke discussion about human survival, environmental degradation, and the cyclical nature of life and death.

---

1. Flood Myths as Archetypes in Storytelling

Flood myths are among the **oldest archetypes** in human storytelling. Across cultures, they often share certain common elements:

- **Divine Wrath or Judgment**: A powerful force (often divine or supernatural) sends a flood to cleanse the world of corruption or evil.
- **Survival**: A lone survivor or a small group of people are spared from the flood, usually because of their righteousness or piety.
- **Rebirth and Renewal**: After the floodwaters recede, the survivors are tasked with repopulating and rebuilding the world, often as part of a divine mandate.

These elements make flood myths incredibly adaptable to different times and settings, making them a staple in popular culture. They tap into universal fears and hopes, such as the fear of annihilation and the hope of survival and renewal. The appeal of these myths is timeless because they speak to the deepest aspects of the human experience.

2. Flood Myths in Cinema: The Big Screen's Take on Cataclysmic Deluge

Flood-based movies often follow a simple narrative arc: a disaster of biblical proportions strikes, submerging cities, destroying civilizations, and forcing the few survivors to rebuild society. While these films may not always directly reference ancient flood myths, they clearly draw inspiration from them. Here are a few notable examples:

a. *Noah* (2014)

Darren Aronofsky's *Noah*, starring Russell Crowe, is a modern reimagining of the Biblical flood story from the book of Genesis. The film retains much of the core elements of the **Noah's Ark** myth: divine judgment, the building of the ark, and the eventual rebirth of humanity after the floodwaters recede. The movie also introduces a fantastical element with **watchers** (giant fallen angels), blending mythology with biblical storytelling to create a visually stunning and philosophical narrative about humanity's sins, redemption, and survival.

b. *2012* (2009)

Roland Emmerich's disaster film *2012* takes the flood myth to an extreme, with a global catastrophe that submerges most of the world's major cities due to rapid melting of the polar ice caps and the breakdown of the Earth's crust. The film features an archetypal "survivalist" story, with a select group of survivors escaping the disaster in massive arks built by world governments. The plot plays on the **apocalyptic fears** of the 21st century, drawing on the flood myth to depict humanity's attempt to survive a cataclysmic event.

c. *The Day After Tomorrow* (2004)

While *The Day After Tomorrow* is more focused on extreme weather and climate change rather than a direct flood, the idea of global devastation and environmental catastrophe mirrors the essence of flood myths. As global warming triggers rapid climate shifts, massive storms and floods devastate the planet, leading to the near-collapse of civilization. This film is a prime example of how flood mythology is intertwined with modern concerns about environmental degradation and the role of humanity in preserving the planet.

d. *Waterworld* (1995)

Waterworld, starring Kevin Costner, is another post-apocalyptic film in which flood and water-based imagery dominate. Set in a world where polar ice caps have melted, flooding much of the Earth's surface, the movie explores a society that has adapted to living on the ocean. In many ways, *Waterworld* echoes the **flood myth** in its setting, where the remnants of humanity must figure out how to survive in a flooded world. The film portrays the sea as both a destructive force and a vital source of survival, emphasizing humanity's resilience in the face of disaster.

---

3. Flood Myths in Literature: Rewriting Ancient Themes

Flood myths also have a prominent place in **literature**, where they continue to be reimagined and adapted to fit contemporary concerns and storytelling formats. Writers often use the flood motif to explore ideas about **society, religion, environmentalism,** and **human hubris**.

a. *The Epic of Gilgamesh* (Translated Texts)

Although the *Epic of Gilgamesh* was written millennia ago, it has continued to inspire authors and poets through the ages. The story of **Utnapishtim**, the Babylonian survivor of the flood, bears striking resemblance to the Biblical Noah and is a significant influence on later flood myths. Modern writers often revisit Utnapishtim's tale to explore themes of immortality, the fleeting nature of civilization, and the relationship between humanity and the divine.

b. *The Flood* by David Maine (2004)

David Maine's novel *The Flood* is a fictional retelling of the story of Noah's Ark from the perspective of the people involved. The book expands on the Biblical account by exploring the emotions and struggles of Noah, his family, and the animals they saved from the flood. By giving depth to the characters, Maine brings a human perspective to the flood myth, reflecting on themes of faith, survival, and the morality of divine punishment.

c. *Oryx and Crake* by Margaret Atwood (2003)

In Atwood's dystopian novel *Oryx and Crake*, the narrative includes a **biological disaster** that wipes out humanity, and while it's not a literal flood, it functions similarly in the way it represents the **collapse of civilization** and the possibility of rebirth. The character Snowman, the protagonist, reflects on the collapse of society and the ethical implications of human interference with nature. It is a modern, speculative take on themes rooted in ancient flood myths—the destruction of a flawed civilization and the possibility of renewal.

d. *Life as We Knew It* by Susan Beth Pfeffer (2006)

This young adult novel, part of the *Moon Crash* series, imagines a **global catastrophe** where the moon shifts orbit and causes global floods. The protagonists, a family, must survive in the aftermath of environmental destruction. The novel's focus on survival in the face of extreme natural disaster draws from the same core idea found in many ancient flood myths: humanity's struggle to survive in a world that is quickly changing and becoming increasingly inhospitable.

---

4. Flood Myths in Video Games: Virtual Dystopias and Survival

Floods, and by extension apocalyptic events, are common themes in the world of **video games**, where players often find themselves in a flooded world or tasked with surviving a rising tide of disaster.

a. *BioShock Infinite* (2013)

While not about literal floods, the plot of *BioShock Infinite* contains symbolic elements tied to **floods of the mind**, power, and revolution. The game's story of a floating city, Columbia, teetering on the brink of collapse touches on the themes of destruction and rebirth that are central to flood myths. The protagonist, Booker DeWitt, must navigate this world of submerged cities, much like the survivors of ancient floods must navigate the post-cataclysmic world.

b. *The Last of Us* (2013)

The Last of Us is set in a post-apocalyptic world where the Earth has been ravaged by a viral outbreak. While it doesn't directly reference ancient floods, the decaying world filled with overgrown cities and submerged landscapes mimics the imagery of a world cleansed by water. The game's emphasis on human survival and the rebuilding of civilization in the wake of a great catastrophe aligns with the core themes of the flood myth.

Flood Myths and Environmentalism: Reflection of Modern Concerns

In modern times, the resurgence of interest in flood myths often correlates with **environmental awareness** and the growing concern about **climate change**. Films, books, and media that explore apocalyptic floods often serve as cautionary tales about the consequences of human activity on the planet. They reflect fears about rising sea levels, the devastation of natural disasters, and the potential collapse of human societies due to environmental negligence.

- **Environmental Activism**: Movies like *An Inconvenient Truth* (2006) or the documentary *Before the Flood* (2016) emphasize the urgency of addressing climate change. While they don't present literal floods, the themes of impending global collapse resonate with the core ideas in flood myths, especially the **cleansing of humanity** and the call for a new way of living with nature.

The integration of flood myths into popular culture serves as a reminder of their deep cultural significance. Whether through ancient texts, modern films, video games, or literature, flood myths continue to evolve and adapt to the concerns of each new generation. The **symbolism** of floods as both a destructive and regenerative force taps into profound questions about survival, environmental stewardship, and humanity's role in the world. Flood myths are not just relics of the past; they continue to shape our narratives and perspectives, providing us with both warnings and hope for the future.

Chapter 70: Conclusion: The Great Floods as a Warning for the Future

The ancient flood myths, which span across cultures and epochs, serve not only as powerful stories of **destruction and survival** but also as poignant metaphors for the fragility of human civilization in the face of **overwhelming natural forces**. From the **Biblical Noah's Ark** to the **Sumerian Epic of Gilgamesh**, these myths often feature divine or cosmic floods that wipe out civilizations, leaving only a few survivors to repopulate the Earth. In many ways, the enduring presence of these myths speaks to humanity's collective consciousness about the **cyclical nature of destruction and rebirth** and the vulnerability of our societies to the forces of nature.

As we reflect on the **connection between ancient flood stories** and modern concerns about **climate change** and **global disasters**, we see that the same themes of environmental upheaval, survival, and renewal resonate powerfully in our current global context. The myths of the great floods may have originated in a time long past, but they continue to offer **timeless insights** into how humanity might respond to the crises we face today.

---

1. Ancient Myths as Reflections of Real Environmental Events

Many of the ancient flood myths appear to have been inspired by real, cataclysmic events in prehistory, such as the **Younger Dryas impact hypothesis**, which proposes that a comet or meteorite strike caused abrupt climate change, global flooding, and mass extinctions. Evidence suggests that these kinds of events may have been burned into the collective memories of ancient peoples, and over generations, the memory of these disasters was passed down through oral traditions, eventually crystallizing into the flood myths we recognize today.

These stories, though often embellished with supernatural elements, can be seen as **cautionary tales** about the devastating potential of natural disasters. The great floods described in these myths were not only a warning of the destructive power of nature but also a reminder of the fragility of human existence. Today, we face similar risks, though not from divine retribution but from the consequences of **climate change, environmental degradation**, and **unsustainable human activity**.

---

2. The Relevance of Flood Myths in the Age of Climate Change

In the 21st century, the **global environmental crisis** has brought a sense of urgency to the themes of destruction and renewal found in ancient flood myths. **Climate change**, driven by human activities such as burning fossil fuels and deforestation, is causing unprecedented shifts in weather patterns, rising sea levels, and more frequent natural disasters, including floods, hurricanes, and droughts.

These environmental changes parallel the **devastating floods** of ancient mythology, reminding us that nature is not only a source of life but also a force capable of massive destruction when pushed to its limits. As cities around the world experience **coastal flooding** due to rising sea levels, and as ecosystems around the globe face collapse, the warning embedded in these myths becomes increasingly clear: humanity must respect the natural world or risk facing the consequences of its own hubris.

Flood myths, especially those that depict survivors rebuilding a better world after the waters recede, may offer hope. They suggest that, after a cataclysm, there is potential for renewal—a chance to start anew and to **reimagine civilization** in harmony with nature rather than in opposition to it. Just as Noah and Utnapishtim were tasked with preserving life in their ark, modern society must find ways to preserve and protect life on Earth. This can only be achieved through sustainable practices and a collective effort to mitigate the environmental damage we have caused.

---

3. The Psychological and Cultural Impact of Flood Myths

The persistence of flood myths in human culture underscores a **psychological** and **cultural understanding** that floods are more than just a metaphor for natural disasters; they represent **existential threats** to human survival and the continuity of civilization. In these myths, floods often serve as a **reset button**, forcing humanity to confront its weaknesses, adapt, and rebuild from the ground up.

In a world where environmental disasters are becoming more frequent and intense, these myths may help shape how modern societies **perceive** and **respond** to climate crises. The **universal appeal** of flood myths, with their themes of destruction and survival, could be harnessed to inspire action in the face of contemporary challenges. Just as the survivors in these myths learned valuable lessons about their relationship with the environment, so too must we learn to live in balance with the Earth, recognizing the interconnectedness of all living beings and the land they inhabit.

4. The Role of Science and Technology in Preventing a Modern-Day Flood

While **ancient societies** had no knowledge of the scientific principles behind climate change or global disasters, modern **science and technology** give us powerful tools to prevent and mitigate the kinds of cataclysms depicted in flood myths. The knowledge accumulated by scientists studying **climate change, oceanography, geology**, and **meteorology** can help us predict and even prevent the worst consequences of rising sea levels, extreme weather, and other environmental hazards.

However, the ability to prevent or mitigate these disasters depends on **global cooperation** and a shift toward sustainable development. Ancient flood myths suggest that a **cataclysm** can only be survived by those who are **prepared**, either through divine favor or human ingenuity. In the case of modern humanity, preparedness means addressing **climate change** through **policy reform, technological innovation**, and **individual action**. Just as the ark in the flood myths was a vessel for survival, today's "ark" could take the form of renewable energy systems, sustainable farming practices, and global efforts to reduce emissions and preserve ecosystems.

---

5. Ethical and Moral Lessons: The Need for Global Responsibility

The story of the **Great Flood** in many cultures carries an ethical and moral lesson: **humanity's survival depends on respecting the natural order.** Whether it is Noah's righteousness, Utnapishtim's wisdom, or the moral lessons of other flood myths, the survivors of the great floods are often those who understand their place within the broader context of the world.

In a world facing **global warming** and **environmental destruction**, we too must learn the moral lesson embedded in these stories: that the fate of humanity is intertwined with the fate of the Earth. Climate change is not just an environmental issue; it is an **ethical issue** that requires us to reconsider how we live on the planet and how we can **share its resources** responsibly. The warning of the flood myths is clear: we cannot continue to exploit the Earth's resources without consequences. There is a moral imperative to **change our ways** before we reach the point of no return.

6. Rebuilding a New World: The Opportunity for a Fresh Start

The post-flood world in many myths is one of **rebirth** and **renewal**. After the floodwaters recede, humanity is given a second chance to build a better, more harmonious world. In the context of modern society, we have the unique opportunity to **rebuild** the world in ways that are more **sustainable, inclusive,** and **environmentally responsible.**

This rebuilding process, however, requires a collective effort to rethink everything from how we produce food to how we consume energy. It calls for a **global reimagining** of economic systems, urban planning, and environmental conservation. Just as the survivors in flood myths must work together to repopulate the Earth, humanity today must work together to ensure a future where **life thrives** in balance with nature.

The flood myths of ancient civilizations remain a powerful **warning** about the vulnerability of human societies to environmental forces. As we face the reality of **climate change**, rising sea levels, and natural disasters, the ancient stories remind us that we are not separate from nature but part of a larger, interconnected system. These myths call us to **reflect on our relationship with the Earth**, and to take action before it is too late.

In many ways, these myths are not just stories of the past—they are **blueprints for the future**, offering lessons on survival, responsibility, and the necessity of **living in harmony** with the environment. The great floods of mythology are not simply the end of the world, but an opportunity for a **new beginning.** The question is: will we heed the warning, or will we repeat the mistakes of the past? The future is in our hands, and the flood myth remains a timeless reminder that we must choose wisely.

Printed in Dunstable, United Kingdom